The Hidden Gem of The Subbética

A Concise History of Priego de Córdoba

The Hidden Gem of The Subbética
A Concise History of Priego de Córdoba

PETER SUCH

THE CHOIR PRESS

Copyright © 2024 Peter Such

All rights reserved. No part of this publication may be reproduced or transmitted in any form or by any means, electronic or mechanical including photocopying, recording or any information storage or retrieval system, without prior permission in writing from the publishers.

The right of Peter Such to be identified as the author of this work has been asserted by him in accordance with the Copyright, Designs and Patents Act 1988

First published in the United Kingdom in 2024 by
The Choir Press

ISBN 978-1-78963-435-8

To the people of Priego de Córdoba, and in particular its historians, poets, teachers and students, with our deep gratitude for the warm welcome that they gave us during the twelve years we spent in their town.

Contents

∽

Preface	ix
Acknowledgements	xi
List of maps	xiii
Chronology	xv
1. Beginnings	1
2. Madīnat Bāguh	19
3. Christendom Victorious	32
4. The Forging of Priego	48
5. Baroque Splendour	66
6. Poverty and Prosperity, Reform and Reaction	92
7. The Tempestuous Decade	125
8. Colossus with Feet of Clay	138
9. Meeting New Challenges	157
Postscript: Priego, Past, Present and Future	180
Select Bibliography	188
Index to Names of People and Places	195

Preface

This book is the product of some twelve years living in one of Priego's villages. It is an expression of my close attachment to the town and of the affection that I feel for its people. However, it also reflects not only Priego's triumphs and glories but also the difficulties and concerns which have accompanied them over the centuries and which continue to do so. My intention has been to provide a concise and accessible introduction to Priego's past, set in the context of that of Spain as a whole and with the aim of examining how the town's history relates to its character as we know it today. Of the rich and extensive literature produced by Priego's historians, very little is available in English and not all of it is easy to obtain. The present volume is directed at the reader who, for whatever reason, has not had the time or the opportunity to gain access to what has been written in Spanish. It is hoped that this will include the numerous English-speaking residents of Priego and its villages as well as readers with a broader interest in Andalusian history. Quotations from Spanish texts and interviews have been given in English translation rather than in the original; in all cases, the translation is my own.

I am all too aware that it is presumptuous of me to claim the authority to write about a town whose past has already been charted by so many outstanding scholars whose knowledge and understanding of the subject is much more intimate and detailed than my own. My debt to them and my profound respect for the quality of their work should be in evidence throughout this book. I am deeply grateful for the help and the encouragement that they have given me and for their patience and generosity. I hope that I have been able to do them justice.

The Hidden Gem of the Subbética

It is only in the relatively recent past that Priego de Córdoba has possessed its present name. For almost six centuries it was known by that given to it by its Muslim inhabitants, which is recorded in various forms, among them 'Medina Bahiga' and, the form that will be used in this book, 'madīnat Bāguh'. After the town's conquest by the Christian armies, it appears in documents as 'Pego' or 'Pliego', which rapidly evolved into the modern version, 'Priego'. This is not the only Priego which exists in Spain, however. There is another town of the same name in the province of Cuenca, and by the late eighteenth century we find our town alluded to as 'Priego de Andalucía', presumably to distinguish it from its namesake. It is not known for certain when it became 'Priego de Córdoba'. This may have been during an administrative reorganisation during the early 1820s, when the province of Córdoba first came into existence. However, the first firm evidence of the use of this name dates from 1883 and it seems to have been only in the 1920s that it was definitively adopted by the town council.[1]

A distinctive feature of Priego is that it includes within its municipal area a total of twenty-five *aldeas* and *diseminados*, that is to say villages and small rural communities. It is beyond the scope of the present volume to give an account of the individual development of each of these. Some of them merit a separate work, as in the case with Miguel Forcada's recent detailed study of Zamoranos. Inevitably, I have dwelt on the history of the town of Priego itself, although I hope that it is made clear that the town's past – as well as its future – is tightly bound in with that of its villages. Perhaps in due course they will become the subject of a volume of their own.

El Poleo, June 2023

---

[1] Alcalá Ortiz, 1988, pp.6–7.

Acknowledgements

The author is deeply indebted to Priego's historians and chroniclers, who have worked with such dedication to make widely available a wealth of information about their town's past. In particular, warm thanks are due to Manuel Peláez del Rosal and Rafael Carmona Ávila for their time and their advice, and to Miguel Forcada Serrano, without whose support and encouragement this book would not have been written. Liz Langdon-Davies played an invaluable part by drawing the maps and by making numerous helpful observations on the text, and photographer Antonio Jesús Villena Martínez gave generously of his time and expertise. I am also very grateful for the assistance given in numerous ways by Antonio Alcalá Ortiz, Félix Javier Serrano Serrano, Félix Serrano Matilla, José Peláez López, Felipe Burgos Sánchez, Casimira Muñoz Povedano and José Pulido Expósito, by the highly efficient team at The Choir Press and – by no means least – by my infinitely patient and supportive wife, Sylvia.

List of Maps

∽∽

Priego de Córdoba today	xxiv
The Priego area in prehistory and until the beginning of the Islamic period	xxvi
Madīnat Bāguh: Priego de Córdoba during the Islamic period	18
Priego de Córdoba at the beginning of the nineteenth century	90

All maps were drawn by Liz Langdon-Davies.

Chronology

∞

Middle Paleolithic: before about 30,000 BC	Evidence of human (Neanderthal) occupation close to river Salado and in the Cueva de Cholones.
End of the Paleolithic period: between 14,000 and 6,000 BC	Human occupation of El Pirulejo; possible human presence in the Cueva de los Mármoles.
Sixth millennium BC	Evidence of a possible agricultural settlement near to the present-day village of Zamoranos.
Neolithic period: from about 4,500 BC	Habitation of caves in the Priego area, including the Cueva de los Mármoles and the Cueva de la Murcielaguina.
Until about 3,000 BC	Evidence of more permanent human habitation and activity in and around caves; growth of settlements above ground.
Approximately 4,000 BC	Earliest evidence of human habitation in the present urban area of Priego (El Palenque).
Between 3,500 and 3,000 BC	Burial site in caves at Las Lagunillas.
Third millennium BC	Bell-beaker pottery at site near El Esparragal.
Towards 2,000 BC	Evidence of Copper Age habitation within present-day urban area of Priego.
From about 1,500 BC	Caves increasingly used for burial rather than for habitation.
From about 1,000 BC	Development of hill-top settlements such as Las Cabezuelas (El Tarajal) and Torre Alta (El Cañuelo).
From about 600 BC	Iberian town of El Cerro de las Cabezas (Fuente-Tójar).
About 300 BC	Settlement on El Cerro de la Cruz (Almedinilla).
About 50–150 AD	Establishment of the Roman villa within the present urban area of Priego.

Chronology

By about 500 AD	Most of the Iberian Peninsula controlled by the Visigoths.
From 711 AD	Invasion of the Peninsula by Islamic armies, collapse of the Visigothic kingdom and imposition of Muslim control.
745	Possible reference to presence of Syrian troops in Bāguh.
756	'Abd al Raḥmān I, as ruler of Muslim Spain, establishes Umayyad emirate in Córdoba.
863	Bāguh is recorded as contributing troops to Muḥammad I's military campaign; the town of madīnat Bāguh is now the centre of a kūra (administrative district).
886	Bāguh becomes involved in the rebellion of 'Umar ibn Ḥafṣūn against the Córdoba emirate.
889	Sa'īd ibn Walid ibn Mastana establishes himself as governor of Bāguh, independent of Córdoba. His family continues to hold power for the next thirty years.
Late ninth or early tenth century	Bāguh is integrated into the administrative area of Elvira.
912–61	In Córdoba 'Abd al Raḥmān III rules over Muslim Spain (from 929 as independent caliph).
921–22	Key strongholds in the area of Bāguh are captured; end of the period of dominance by Mastani's descendants.
929	'Abd al Raḥmān III appoints a new governor to Bāguh, which is now independent of Elvira.
974	Bāguh again listed as a territory of Elvira.
1008–10	A period of civil war leads to the dissolving of the Umayyad caliphate.
1013	Zirid dynasty establishes **taifa** kingdom of Granada, of which Bāguh is part.

CHRONOLOGY

1073	Madīnat Bāguh is the scene of negotiations between representatives of the Christian rulers of Castile-León and the Muslim kingdom of Seville.
1090	The taifa kingdom of Granada is conquered by the north African Almoravid invaders; madīnat Bāguh comes under Almoravid control.
1147	Almohad invaders enter the Iberian Peninsula. Under their rule, madīnat Bāguh enjoys its period of greatest growth and prosperity.
1212	A Christian army under Alfonso VIII of Castile routs the Almohads at Las Navas de Tolosa.
1225	Christian armies under Fernando III capture mādinat Bāguh and the castle is razed to the ground.
1220s?	Priego is reoccupied by Muslims.
1246	The town is retaken by Fernando III and given to the Order of Calatrava.
By 1332	Priego is again part of the Muslim kingdom of Granada.
1341	Alfonso XI retakes the town and from now on it remains part of the kingdom of Castile-León.
1377	The lordship of Priego is granted to Gonzalo Fernández de Córdoba.
1406–07	Priego is unsuccessfully besieged by Islamic forces.
1426	Establishment in Priego of the Cofradía de San Ildefonso.
1427– approximately 1441	The king's favourite Álvaro de Luna is responsible for the defence of Priego.
1455–1501	Don Alfonso de Aguilar (Alfonso Fernández de Córdoba) holds lordship of Priego.
1485	First known settlement of Morisco families in Priego.
1492	The city of Granada is surrendered to the Christian armies, led by the 'Catholic Monarchs'.

Chronology

1501	Creation of the Marquisate of Priego. Pedro Fernández de Córdoba III is named Marquis of Priego on the death in battle of his father, Don Alfonso.
1510	Foundation in Priego of the convent of San Esteban.
1516–56	The Habsburg Carlos I becomes king of Spain.
1517	Pedro Fernández de Córdoba III dies and is succeeded by his daughter Doña Catalina Fernández de Córdoba.
1520	Establishment of the Cofradía de la Limpia Concepción de la Virgen María.
1525	Work begins on the construction of the church of La Asunción.
1549	Completion of the church of San Francisco.
1550	Foundation of the Cofradía de la Vera Cruz.
1556–98	Felipe II king of Spain.
1560s	Foundation of the Colegio de San Nicasio.
From 1566	Bullfights held in El Palenque square.
1568	Morisco uprising in the Alpujarras.
1520	New municipal buildings in El Llano.
1572–76	Construction of El Pósito.
1586	Completion of La Fuente de la Salud.
1593	Foundation of the Hermandad de Jesús Nazareno. Origins of the May processions.
1611	Expulsion of all Moriscos from Spain.
1621	Priego purchases for 130,000 ducados the right to administer the alcabala or sales tax.
1637	Foundation of Hospital de San Onofre (later San Juan de Dios).
1641	The town of Priego is required to send men of noble birth to fight against Catalan and Portuguese rebels.
About 1642	Initial foundation of the Hermandad de Jesús en la Columna and beginning of the May processions.

Chronology

1664	Discalced Franciscans move to chapel of San Pedro and work begins on new church.
1680	Town buildings damaged by earthquake; outbreak of plague; economic crisis following years of poor harvests.
1700	Death of Carlos II and succession to the throne of Felipe V, Spain's first Bourbon monarch.
1705	Priego contributes troops for the defence of Cádiz.
1709	Adoption of the Immaculate Conception as Priego's patron, alongside San Nicasio.
1735	Widespread starvation in the province of Córdoba.
1744–78	Construction of the church of La Aurora.
1750–90	Silk production in Priego reaches its peak but by the following decade has begun to decline. The programme of construction and embellishment of ecclesiastical buildings is at its height.
1784	Completion of the Sagrario in the church of La Asunción.
Approximately 1790	The debt for the alcabala is finally repaid.
1800–02	Construction of La Fuente del Rey.
1808	Abdication of Carlos IV and French invasion of Spain.
1810	French troops occupy Priego.
1814	With French armies expelled, Fernando VII re-enters Spain.
1820–23	'Liberal Triennium': liberal administration in Priego proposes programme of reforms.
1823	Fernando VII re-establishes absolutist rule. Outside Priego, confrontation between Generals Riego and Ballesteros.
1833	Death of Fernando VII, who is succeeded by three-year-old Isabel II. First Carlist War begins.
1835	Friars expelled from convents of San Esteban (San Francisco) and San Pedro.

Chronology

1837	New liberal constitution; abolition of seignorial jurisdiction; Priego freed from feudal control by dukes of Medinaceli. Villages of Almedinilla, Fuente Tójar and (temporarily) Castil de Campos given autonomous status.
1868	Successful national uprising against Isabel II; establishment of a revolutionary committee in Priego; seizure of the Clarist convent of San Antonio.
By approximately 1870	Cotton textiles are being produced in Priego.
1874	Re-establishment of the Bourbon monarchy under Alfonso XII; in Priego Carlists submit to authorities.
1881	Priego granted the status of 'ciudad'.
1885	Damage caused by earthquake; torrential storms; Priego threatened by cholera epidemic.
1892	Installation of the telegraph in Priego; official opening of the new bull-ring.
1902	Establishment of factory using hydro-electric power in Las Angosturas.
Approximately 1905	Electric power available in Priego urban area.
1915	Installation of the telephone; foundation of the newspaper 'Patria Chica' (lasts for seven months).
1917	Niceto Alcalá-Zamora appointed national Minister for Development.
1918	General strike of Priego workers.
1923	Military coup by Miguel Primo de Rivera leads to establishment of dictatorship: in Priego José Tomás Valverde becomes mayor, implementing an extensive programme of improvement in the town's infrastructure.
January 1930	End of dictatorship: Primo de Rivera resigns and leaves Spain.
14th April 1931	In Priego, the valverdistas are victorious in the municipal elections.

Chronology

16th April 1931	Alfonso XIII goes into exile. The result of municipal elections won by the right, including in Priego, is declared void.
December 1931	Niceto Alcalá-Zamora declared President of the Second Republic.
August 1932	Attempted coup by General Sanjurjo. José Tomás Valverde is imprisoned for complicity.
Academic year 1933–34	Alcalá-Zamora Secondary School is opened.
April 1936	Niceto Alcalá-Zamora dismissed from his post as President of the Second Republic.
17th–18th July 1936	Nationalist uprising and outbreak of civil war; in Priego, members of the Falange combine to take control.
22nd July 1936	José Tomás Valverde arrives in Priego.
4th August 1936	The town council is officially replaced by a new 'municipal management committee'.
August 1936	Failure of Republicans' attempt to take Córdoba.
September 1937	Permanent closure of Alcalá-Zamora Secondary School
October 1937	Bombs fall on Priego (and also El Cañuelo and Zagrilla).
1st April 1939	Surrender of Republican forces. General Franco declares the Civil War at an end.
1945	Founding of olive oil cooperative 'La Purísima'.
1948 (until 1970)	Establishment of training school/workshop in Priego for employees in the cotton industry.
From August 1948	Annual festival of music and song.
1952	Completion and opening of new town hall.
1953	Foundation of the periodical **Adarve**.
1953–54	Opening of Instituto Fernando III el Santo.
1957	Establishment of homes for the elderly by Fundación Arjona Valera and Fundación Mármol.
1957	Opening of the cinema 'Cine Gran Capitán'; establishment of new factory of 'Hilaturas del Carmen'.

Chronology

1959	Introduction of the national Stabilisation Plan.
1961	'Atlético Prieguense' wins promotion to the national football league.
1961	Plan for seventeen factories to amalgamate into a single business.
1963	Production by Priego's textile industry is at its peak.
1966	CEPANSA (National Cotton Production Company) introduces plan for restructuring.
1967	Scheme for restructuring of textile industry finally abandoned.
1972	Since 1966, twenty-six of Priego's cotton mills have closed.
1975	Death of General Franco.
1980	Opening of the Peña Flamenca.
By 1981	In the past thirty years, Priego's population has decreased by over a quarter.
1985	Opening of the health centre; plans published for the opening of the A-339 to connect Priego with Lucena/Cabra and Alcalá La Real.
January 1986	Spain becomes a full member of the European Union.
Early 1990s	Work begins on the industrial estate at La Vega.
1992	Provisional approval obtained for denominación de origen for olive oils from the Priego area.
1993	Opening of new sports centres in Castil de Campos and Zamoranos.
1995	Opening in Zagrilla of the hotel complex known as la villa turística de Priego; announcement of plans for the development of the Palenque complex.
1998	Protests by olive oil producers against quotas introduced by the European Union.
1999	Inauguration of the Museo Adolfo Lozano Sidro.
2001	Seven cooperatives combine to market olive oil as Almazaras de la Subbética.
2007	Opening of the public library.

Chronology

2011	Inauguration of new secondary school, Carmen Pantión.
2012	The Hospedería San Francisco opens in the old convent buildings.
2016	Opening to the public of the Recreo de Castilla gardens.
2017	Opening of the new indoor food market.
2018–19	Opening of the Hotel-Museo Patria Chica.
2020	New civil guard barracks comes into operation; Priego's Carlos Machado wins the national table tennis championship for the eleventh time in twenty years.
2021	Since 2004, Rincón de la Subbética olive oil has won over 500 awards worldwide.
2023	Completion of the redevelopment of Calle Río.

Priego de Córdola today

Places of interest

1. Paseo del Adarve: walkway around the perimeter of the walled area
2. Iglesia (church) de Nuestra Señora de la Asunción
3. Castle
4. Recreo de Castilla: gardens named after the Castilla family
5. Montoro-Castilla family mill: projected site of new museum
6. Carnicerías Reales: historic municipal meat market and slaughterhouse
7. Paseo de Colombia
8. Iglesia de la Aurora
9. Iglesia y convento de San Francisco: the restored convent is now a hotel
10. Pabellón de Deportes: sports pavilion
11. Ermita de Belén
12. Mercado de Abastos: food market
13. Iglesia de San Pedro Apóstol
14. Iglesia de San Juan de Díos
15. Ayuntamiento (town hall) and tourist office
16. Iglesia de Nuestra Señora de las Angustias
17. Birthplace of Niceto Alcalá-Zamora
18. Iglesia de Nuestra Señora del Carmen
19. Teatro Victoria
20. Museum of municipal history in the Adolfo Lozano-Sidro cultural centre
21. Iglesia de las Mercedes
22. Hotel-Museo Patria Chica
23. Plaza Palenque: municipal offices and public library
24. Correos: post office
25. Ermita del Calvario
26. Iglesia de la Trinidad
27. Public health centre
28. Bus station
29. Fundación Residencia Arjona Valera: residence for the elderly
30. Plaza de Toros: the bull ring
31. Ciudad Deportiva Carlos Machado: sporting complex
32. Albasur: centre for the disabled
33. Atarazana district: area designated for redevelopment
34. Municipal park and exhibition centre, named after Niceto Alcalá-Zamora
35. Los Almendros: residential area
36. Civil guard barracks

Navigational references

A. Barrio de la Villa
B. Plaza de Andalucia: connected to Fuente del Rey by way of Calle Río
C. Plaza de la Constitución
D. Fuente del Rey (and Fuente de la Salud)
E. Plaza El Palenque: connected to Plaza de la Constitución by way of Calle Carrera de la Monjas

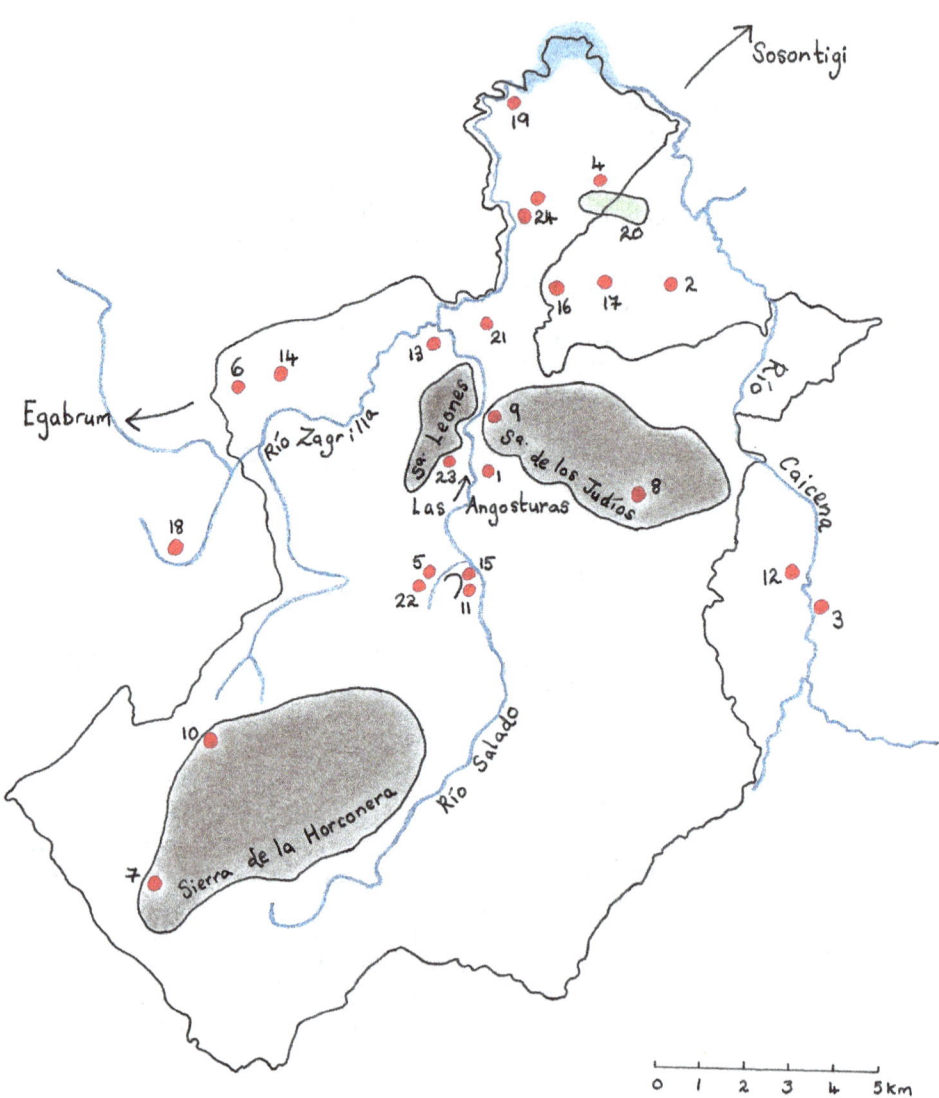

The Priego area in prehistory and until the beginning of the Islamic period

1 Azores
2 Cerro de las Cabezas
3 Cerro de la Cruz
4 Cerro Lucerico
5 Copper Age Site
6 Cueva de Cholones
7 Cueva de las Cuarenta
8 Cueva de los Mármoles
9 Cueva de la Murcielaguina, and close to this, Cueva de Huerta Anguita
10 El Arrimadizo
11 El Pirulejo
12 El Ruedo (Roman Villa near the present-day town of Almedinilla)
13 El Tarajal – showing a flat-topped hill above the village
14 El Villar de Zagrilla
15 Escarpment: edge of the travertine platform on which the present-day town of Priego stands
16 Fuente de la Salud, in the present-day village of El Cañuelo
17 Iliturgicola
18 Ipolcobulcoba
19 Los Castillejos
20 Los Llanos, outside the present-day village of Zamoranos
21 Torre Alta
22 Roman Villa discovered near the site of the present-day town hall in Priego
23 Roman Villa recently discovered at the site of El Cortijo de los Cipreses
24 Zamoranos – elevated points above the present-day village of Zamoranos, where evidence of above-ground Neolithic settlements has been found

CHAPTER 1

Beginnings

֍

The town now known as Priego de Córdoba lies within the Cordillera Subbética (or Sierras Subbéticas), a mountain system which runs across southern Spain from Cape Trafalgar in the west as far as the present-day province of Murcia in the east. Today, the term 'Subbética' is applied specifically to a rugged semi-mountainous area in the south of the province of Córdoba, which contains peaks such as those of the Sierra Horconera, most notably La Tiñosa, at 1,570 metres the highest in the province of Córdoba.[2] Some 10 kilometres from La Tiñosa sits the town of Priego, situated on a platform of travertine (a kind of limestone), on the edge of an escarpment which forms a natural fortification facing towards the east. This is karstic limestone country with characteristic features such as the gorge at Las Angosturas through which the A333 now winds its way northwards towards Jaén. There are also underground caverns and an abundance of natural springs.

It is not surprising that earliest evidence of habitation in the area should be found either on the banks of its rivers or in caves. Simple flint tools belonging to the Middle Paleolithic period, to the Neanderthal Mousterian culture, which developed between 90,000 and 30,000 years ago, have been discovered in a number of sites. Probably the most important of these is located on the bank of the river Salado on the slopes of the hill now known as the Cerro de las Viñas, in the Sierra de Albayate.

---

[2] *Hispania Baetica* was the southernmost of the three provinces into which the Romans divided the Iberian Peninsula. Its title was derived from *Baetis*, the name which they gave to the river Guadalquivir.

It was for a long time considered that the most important evidence of very early human habitation had been discovered in the Cueva de los Mármoles or Cave of the Marbles, a complex of caves situated in the hills known as the Sierra de los Judíos (literally the Hills of the Jews), about 7 kilometres north-east of the present-day Priego. This conclusion was based principally on a stone-scraping implement argued by some scholars to date from the Mousterian period. However, it is now accepted that the material found there was considerably later in origin.[3] Nevertheless, the Cueva de los Mármoles, apart from offering a multi-coloured spectacle of extreme beauty, is of immense archaeological interest. Discoveries in different parts of the complex have pointed to occupation at various points dating back as far as the end of the Upper Paleolithic period (about 10,000 BC) and stretching as far forward as the period of Islamic occupation at the end of the first millennium AD.

In the Cueva de la Murcielaguina, which lies close to the point where, 6 kilometres north of Priego, the river Salado passes through the gorge of Las Angosturas, there have been discoveries of animal remains, signs of fire and stone tools and hunting implements, also from the end of the Upper Paleolithic period. And to the north-west, on the outskirts of what is now the village of Zagrilla Alta, a deep and inaccessible part of the Cueva de Cholones contains a collection of cave paintings, also Paleolithic in origin.[4] These paintings include both geometrical forms and representations of animals (goats) and, though schematic in style, of a group of human beings that appear to be engaged in some kind of ceremony or ritual. On the hillock above the caves, known as the Loma de Cholones, the discovery of several items also dating from the final stages of the Paleolithic period is a firm indication that the area was used for the production of flint implements.[5]

---

[3] See Carmona Ávila, Lunes Osuna and Moreno Rosa, 104.

[4] Moreno Rosa, 1992, 22, concludes that the paintings date from the end of the Upper Paleolithic period.

[5] For a fuller account of the importance of this site, see Rubio Valverde, 43–45.

Extensive evidence of early human occupation has also been discovered on the lands of the farm called El Pirulejo, situated just to the east of the present-day town of Priego alongside the A339 as it approaches from Alcalá La Real. The site lies very close to the river Salado, at the foot of the travertine formation on which the oldest part of the town stands. The initial chance discovery of a Bronze Age burial site led to further exploration, and evidence emerged of habitation in the much older Magdalenian period (between 14,000 and 6,000 BC), when the area would have been covered by woodland and the climate was wetter and cooler than that of the present day. The material found there includes the finest collection of decorative art from the Upper Paleolithic period that has been discovered anywhere in Andalucía, a rich variety of objects which include numerous stone tools and weapons of high quality, a large number of shells used for decoration (undoubtable evidence of the existence of trade routes) and pieces of sandstone carved with a variety of motifs, among them a picture of a goat's head. There is clear evidence of the construction of some kind of roofing fixed by posts to the ground and of a small stone wall.

El Pirulejo is a site of outstanding importance, although today part of it lies buried under the A339 and the remainder is in a state of neglect. There is, however, more evidence elsewhere in the Priego area of the production of flint implements of high quality during the Upper Paleolithic period, notably in the Llano de Vichira at the foot of the mountains of the Sierra de la Horconera, in the south-western part of the municipal area.

The so-called 'Neolithic Revolution' is marked by the transition from hunter-gathering to agriculture and settlement and is generally understood to have occurred in southern Spain between approximately 5,000 and 3,000 BC. Recent research has produced extensive evidence (building materials, pottery, tools, weapons and decorative artefacts, together with a wide variety of animal bones) of a primitive agricultural settlement situated on the hill known as the Cerro del Cercado near the present-day village of Zamoranos, situated some 10 kilometres north of Priego. The settlement could date from the sixth millennium BC, which means that these are among the oldest known man-made structures in Andalucía. At the time of writing, work on this important site continues.

The Neolithic period saw the evolution in south-eastern Spain of what some archaeologists have termed 'the Culture of Caves with Decorated Pottery'. The geology of the area around Priego, with its numerous natural caves and underground passages, was well suited to the growing tendency for humans to settle in permanent communities, domesticating animals which had previously existed in the wild and cultivating cereal crops.[6] Most of the caves show signs of human occupation from about 4,000 BC, but it is the Cueva de los Mármoles which provides the most extensive evidence of habitation. The large range of tools found there suggests that they were manufactured within the cave; one of them appears to have been in regular use in the harvesting of crops and others for the grinding of iron and hematite (found locally) which are used, when mixed with clay, in the decoration of pottery. There is an abundance of items used for personal decoration and of a range of materials, including marble, animal tusks and even seashells, and this is further evidence of trade with coastal areas. In particular, there are several stone bracelets, both finished and in the course of production, and the quantity and the variety of these finds points to the existence of a kind of workshop in the cave.[7] This appears to represent a sporadic and seasonal activity which complemented the herding and pastoral activities by which the cave dwellers lived. In addition, both in the Cueva de los Mármoles and in a number of other caves, there are numerous and varied examples of the red ochre pottery

---

[6] In some parts of the area, however, it seems likely that such activity would have been largely limited to the rearing of sheep and goats. See Carmona Ávila, Lunes Osuna and Moreno Rosa, 107–08.

[7] For a detailed study of the articles produced in this 'workshop' and of the methods of production, see Martínez Sevilla, 38–53.

which is most typical of the Neolithic period, as well as pieces in other decorative styles.

There is ample evidence of human occupation of the Cueva de Cholones during this period, and there can be no doubt that, like the Cueva de los Mármoles, it was used for burials. Moreover, in the hills of la Horconera, near the present-day village of Las Lagunillas, some 10 kilometres south-west of Priego, there has been a more spectacular discovery of a burial site, known as the Cueva de los Cuarenta ('Cave of the Forty'), dating back to the second half of the fourth millennium BC. This cave system contains the skeletal remains of some forty individuals, together with burial goods including pottery, polished and carved stone items and one decorative object made of amber. The last of these in particular seems to be an indication of contact with trade routes.

Mention should be made, too, of the paintings to be found on the walls of several of the caves of the area.[8] Outstanding examples are to be found in the Cueva de la Murcielaguina which, like those in the Cueva de Cholones, are situated in a remote and inaccessible area of the complex. Of those most recently discovered, the most fascinating consists of a series of lines converging on a central point, which could be interpreted as a representation of the sun.

The evidence of human habitation of the area's caves during the Neolithic period points to a relatively advanced economy: in addition to the hunting of large game, there is no doubt that from around 5,000 to 4,000 BC the inhabitants of the area around the present-day town of Priego kept sheep, goats and pigs and that they cultivated wheat and barley. Occupation of the caves was on a regular basis, but perhaps seasonal. The most important cave sites were in the Sierra de los Judíos and near the gorge of Las Angosturas, though numerous others (notably in the Sierra Gallinera, to the west, towards the present-day town of Carcabuey) may well have been inhabited less frequently,

---

[8] See Carmona Ávila, Lunes Osuna and Moreno Rosa, 109.

perhaps by people on the move with livestock. In addition, there is evidence of Neolithic settlements above ground, for example, at a number of elevated points rising above the relatively level terrain on which the present-day village of Zamoranos stands.[9] As we have already seen, one of these sites now appears to date back to a significantly older period. This was an area rich in the iron ore and hematite used for the red ochre pottery, and the material discovered there (a variety of stone and decorative objects as well as pottery) shows that the way of life of its Neolithic inhabitants had much in common with that of the people who have left their traces in the caves.

Although the third millennium BC in Andalucía is generally identified with the so-called Copper Age (also known as the Chalcolithic period), in this relatively inaccessible area of the Subbética, working with metal played very little part and living conditions were very slow to evolve. The centres of habitation remained relatively unchanged, with the caves still of great importance, although there does appear to have been a steady increase in the number of settlements above ground. There is evidence of some work with textiles and also of the presence of simple votive objects. Investigation of the site on the Cerro del Torreón near the present-day village of El Esparragal (7 kilometres to the north of Priego) has pointed to habitation from the end of the Neolithic period but which lasted until an advanced stage of the Copper Age. There are indications of the existence of a basic form of constructed dwelling, and the discovery there of an example of so-called 'bell-beaker' pottery indicates links with more advanced communities.

Until quite recently, little was known about the initial occupation of what is now Priego's urban area. However, since the creation of the municipal Department of Archaeology in 1989, a series of important discoveries has transformed our understanding of the earliest stages of human habitation. In 1995, excavation of an Islamic necropolis in the area now

---

[9] See Forcada Serrano, 2018, 21, and Carmona Ávila, Lunes Osuna and Moreno Rosa, 108.

corresponding to the top of Calle Cava, Calle Tercia and Calle Trasmonjas produced finds of pottery and flint tools and weapons which were considered to date from the Copper Age, towards 2,000 BC. This was believed at the time to be the earliest indication of a human presence in the present urban area. Subsequently, however, a number of sites in the historic area of the Barrio de la Villa and in the modern town centre have provided important new evidence in the form of pottery, tools, weapons and animal bones. In particular, the discoveries in the central part of the town point to human habitation at a much earlier date, and investigation of one grave in the Islamic necropolis on the site corresponding to the present-day square of El Palenque appears to leave little doubt that there was a human presence here (about 250 metres from the source of the river) at some point between the end of the fifth millennium and the beginning of the fourth millennium BC.

By the second millennium BC, the Iberian Peninsula was entering the Bronze Age, as the use of stone progressively gave way to that of metal, which was worked with increasing sophistication. At the same time, societies and settlements began to take on more complex features, and, conspicuously, funeral rites evolved towards individual burials which reflected social status. Contact with more advanced communities in other parts of Andalucía appears to have remained infrequent and indirect. Nevertheless, by about 1,500 BC, a new pattern was being reflected in burial sites such as the one found in the Cueva de Huerta Anguita, which is situated near to the Cueva de la Murcielaguina. Here, the grave goods included a distinctive triangular copper dagger as well as a large sword blade made of flint and a variety of decorative items. And at El Pirulejo, a group of burials also display parallels with the so-called Argar culture originating in the Mediterranean area of south-eastern Spain. By now, caves such as the Cueva de los Mármoles were being much less used for habitation and probably principally for burial. In spite of such changes, however, it is clear that the area that is now Priego was remote from trade routes and lacked the metallic mineral resources which led to more rapid development elsewhere.

In the first half of the first millennium BC, the most significant cultural and economic advances in Andalucía were associated with the metal-rich society of Tartessos based in the south west near the mouth of the river Guadalquivir, whose existence is documented from the beginning of the millennium and which from about 600 BC formed an important trading partnership with the Phoenicians. Undoubtedly, however, our area of the Subbética had little direct contact with these developments. It was very slow to absorb the cultural influences that were bringing greater sophistication in the use of materials, in the production of pottery and in agriculture to other areas of Andalucía. By about the sixth century BC, there are certainly some signs of external links: notably the appearance of decorated pottery, indicating contact with the Tartessian culture, and of bronze arrowheads, which suggest Phoenician influence. At the important sites at Cerro Severo, Torre Alta and Las Cabezuelas del Tarajal, there have been discoveries of pottery with Punic (or Carthaginian) parallels and perhaps even of Punic origin, a further indication of a connection with the coastal region at this early stage. At Las Cabezuelas, there is also important evidence of the growth of a new kind of settlement, the outstanding example of which is the strongly fortified area which stands on a large flat-topped hill rising above the present-day village of El Tarajal.

Nevertheless, in general, what is known of such tendencies is not extensive. In particular, in what is now the Priego urban area, there is no clear evidence of firmly established settlements before the end of the Bronze Age (approximately 850 BC). Here, the limited finds mentioned earlier provide some evidence of habitation but no more than this.

In Spain, the second half of the first millennium BC (and more specifically the period between the fourth century BC and the first century AD) is identified with the so-called Iberian culture. This term was originally used by Greek geographers and applied to the people that the Romans were to call 'Hispani'. Iberian social structure was markedly hierarchical and dominated by a warrior elite, and its people grouped into independent settlements (usually situated on heights dominating the countryside), like the one at Las Cabezuelas. The use of iron weaponry became increasingly common and where metal resources existed these could be used for trade, particularly with merchants from the Mediterranean area. Both Phoenician and Greek colonies were established in coastal regions, and their cultural influence spread steadily. It seems most likely that the area around present-day Priego was dominated by the people that the Romans came to call the Bastetani, who occupied the Subbética, but there was probably also close contact with the Turdetani, whose culture is closely associated with that of Tartessos. It may well be that this area represented a kind of frontier zone between the two peoples, characterised by the hill-top fortifications which controlled the surrounding territory and routes for communication.

There is, however, no evidence that cultural development or structural change in the Subbética area came either rapidly or consistently. The major sites of the Bronze Age such as Las Cabezuelas at El Tarajal retained their importance, and it was only towards the end of the second century BC that Las Cabezuelas was abandoned and superseded as a fortification and population centre by Torre Alta. Torre Alta seems to have become the nerve centre of a group of settlements in the area of the present-day villages of El Cañuelo and Zamoranos, which also includes the Cerro de las Pollicas and Los Llanos. (The word 'cerro' denotes a hill, and in such cases specifically the flat-topped hills particularly suited to settlements which are common in the Priego area.) Torre Alta is situated about one and a half kilometres further north than Las Cabezuelas and, occupying a stronger natural defensive hill-top site, in due course, it was to be surrounded by several rings of walls. Items discovered at Torre Alta, which include bronze arrowheads from the seventh or the sixth century BC, point to contact with the culture of Tartessos or with Phoenician traders, but it was in the Iberian period that this settlement was to achieve much greater prominence. Its distinctive features include, set into the hillside, the tomb of an Iberian warrior, whose ashes had been buried in a funeral urn together with a variety of grave goods.

Such hill-top towns from the Iberian period are known by the Latin term of *oppida*. A particularly striking example is Cerro Severo (or Cebero), which is strategically situated on one of the most important trade routes across the Subbética. In this case, the settlement appears to date back to the first half of the first millennium BC. There is no evidence of the construction of fortifications. What most distinguishes it is the relationship which clearly existed between its inhabitants and the Punic (or Carthaginian) world. Finds made here from the Iberian period include a rich collection of pottery of Punic style or origin and also a large number of Hispano-Carthaginian coins. A variety of objects have been discovered, including a decorated jar used to store herbs or medicines and a container, in the form of a female head, for oil or ointment, which appears to have been based on a Greek original, in turn imitating a model dating back to the seventh century BC.[10]

In addition to such communities, the Iberian period saw the establishment of small fortified areas, sometimes with quite complex defences and situated at strategically important points, which contributed to the protection of the towns. There were several of these in the Priego area, such as Los Castillejos, situated to the north of Fuente-Tójar and which was to remain in use during the period of Roman domination.

Also significant in the Iberian period is the sacred role that was now played by the Cueva de la Murcielaguina, situated in the gorge of Las Angosturas: the sculpture of a human head and the presence of various items of decorated pottery point to the use of the cave for ritual purposes.

It is outside the present-day Priego municipal area that the

---

[10] See Carmona Ávila, Luna Osuna and Moreno Rosa, 117.

most important of the *oppida* of the region are to be found, but they certainly merit our attention for what they tell us of cultural developments during the Iberian period and beyond. The Iberian settlement which stood on the Cerro de la Cruz, rising above what is now the town of Almedinilla, some 12 kilometres to the east of Priego, dates from the third century BC. The settlement occupies a site of about 50,000 square metres and represents a complex urban development on stepped terraces cut into the steep hillsides. There was a network of streets, with housing, workshops and agricultural buildings such as mills and stores. The necropolis contains a wealth of grave goods, notably a wide range of weaponry. The Iberian town seems finally to have been destroyed by a devastating fire towards the end of the second century BC, probably in the course of an attack by an invading Roman force.

The Cerro de las Cabezas, near the present-day town of Fuente-Tójar, some 10 kilometres north-east of Priego, was the site of the Iberian settlement of Iliturgicola. Although there is evidence of habitation on this site going back to the Bronze Age, the Iberian community dates from the sixth century BC, when it was first surrounded by a ring of walls, and it lasted until the second century BC when, like the settlement on the Cerro de la Cruz, it was conquered by the Romans. Iliturgicola's two necropoleis give a sense of the wealth and importance of the town and of its heavily hierarchical society. This was clearly an important agricultural centre and one on which other, smaller, communities depended. There is evidence of contact with Phoenician and subsequently Carthaginian traders. The wealth of finds from the Iberian period includes weapons, sculptures, pottery, cinerary urns, votive and decorative objects and parts of a loom, and it is generally recognised that this important archaeological site still has many secrets to yield up.

The settlements on the Cerro de la Cruz and the Cerro de las Cabezas represented centres of considerable economic and military significance in the period preceding the seizure of control over the region by the Romans. However, there is no such evidence from this period for the area that was going to become the site of the town of Priego.

*

The Romans began their conquest of the Iberian Peninsula at the end of the third century BC, initially as part of their struggle against the Carthaginians. Effectively, they had driven out their opponents by 202 BC, and their period of political control was to last until the fourth century AD. As there was no overarching political organisation, they dealt individually with towns and tribes, giving affiliate Roman status to those who submitted readily to their authority. Their response to those that did not was brutal, and we can only suppose that this was the case with the settlement on the Cerro de la Cruz. Iliturgicola, on the other hand, prospered under Roman rule and in particular it is known to have flourished as a centre for the production and export of olive oil. On the hill known as the Cerro Lucerico there was an industrial complex considered by archaeologists to constitute one of the most important Roman olive oil mills in the Iberian Peninsula.

The Priego area initially formed part of the province of Hispania Ulterior (literally the part of the Peninsula furthest from Rome), but after the reorganisation of 27 BC, it belonged to that of Baetica, whose capital was Corduba (now the city of Córdoba) and, within this, to an administrative region based on the town of Astigis (Écija). On the whole, the pattern of occupation remained largely unchanged, with smaller communities like the fortified *oppida* of Torre Alta and Los Castillejos continuing to exist. Several of the settlements known to have been in existence during the Roman period were on sites already inhabited by the indigenous peoples, although Los Llanos near Zamoranos appears to have been newly established. There was no city within the Priego area, and the nearest towns, as well as Iliturgicola, were Sosontigi (Alcaudete, about 25 kilometres north-east of Priego) and Ipolcobulcoba, which stood on the hilltop now occupied by the castle of Carcabuey (10 kilometres to the west).

It is known that there were a number of small Roman settlements including villas which served as the centre of estates devoted principally to the cultivation of vines, olives and cereals. Among those in which clear evidence has been found of both a residential area and agricultural buildings are the sites at Los Llanos and El Villar de Zagrilla. Evidence of further settlements continues to come to light, notably in the case of the exciting discovery in 2022 of an important complex at El Cortijo de los Cipreses, near the gorge of Las Angosturas, about 2 kilometres north of Priego. Currently in the early stages of investigation, it appears to contain the remains of a fortified villa dating from the first or second century AD and consisting of at least eight buildings. These include residential accommodation, olive mills, storage, fortifications, baths and two streets, altogether covering some 1,650 square metres. The width of the Roman road (over 6 metres) which also forms part of the site indicates that this area was considered to be of considerable importance.

As an outstanding example of a Roman settlement, another villa, that of El Ruedo near Almedinilla, has already been much studied and provides an excellent example of how such settlements would have combined two elements: the dwelling (in this case, a luxurious one) of the owners and also the farm buildings and accommodation for the slaves. In particular, in the Baetica region, the period of Roman domination saw a considerable increase in the production of olive oil, with large quantities exported to Rome itself. The use of the press for the extraction of the oil was already known to the Iberians (it had probably been introduced through the influence of the Phoenicians), but the extent of the land devoted to olive trees appears to have been quite limited up to this point. However, by the first century BC, southern Spain was famous for both the quality and the quantity of the oil that it produced. The techniques for production advanced rapidly, too, and the process used for the elaboration of olive oil would subsequently remain largely unchanged until the introduction of the electrically powered hydraulic press in the 1950s.

On the whole, the process of Romanisation of the Priego area was relatively slow. A key development occurred in 73–74 AD, under the Emperor Vespasian, when the right to Roman citizenship was granted to the province of Hispania and towns of native origin acquired the status of *municipium*, a change which led to an increase in population. A number of new settlements in the Priego area were established, and the total number of these seems at its peak to have reached about twenty, before, from the third century AD, the population once again began to decline.

Outstanding among the surviving architectural features from this period is the Fuente de la Salud ('Fountain of Health'), a stone fountain possibly dedicated to the Naiads (Greek water nymphs). It is situated in El Cañuelo, near to Zamoranos. Items from the time of both the Republic (up to 27 BC) and the Empire (until the fifth century AD) have been found in various parts of the Priego area, including an oven used for the production of bricks and tiles (in Fuente Barea) and a variety of pottery, with numerous examples of the characteristic Roman *terra sigillata* (usually bright red pottery impressed with designs). There are also inscriptions and epitaphs (of which many were produced on the Cerro de las Cabezas), a carved marble torso (Azores), a marble decorative bust (Las Angosturas) and a fragment from a capital (Sierra Leones). Discoveries have also included a variety of metal objects (iron and bronze: weapons, decorative and also household items) and also numerous coins (particularly from the urban settlements of Torre Alta and Cañoscorrientes). Among the Roman burial sites in this area are necropoleis situated near to these two centres. There is also evidence of the extensive use during this period of the caves of the area for a variety of purposes including temporary or permanent habitation, storage, the sheltering of livestock and also as places of worship. The large number of items found in the Cueva de la Murcielaguina indicates that it was used over an extended period between the second century BC and the fourth century AD and that until the beginning of the second century AD this was for religious purposes. It also seems likely that during the later Imperial period some of the caves of the area were used by hermits.

Nevertheless, the overall picture of Roman occupation in the area is limited and, until the beginning of the twenty-first century, it appeared that within the area corresponding to the modern town of Priego itself there was little to point to the existence of any significant level of habitation from that period. Priego, it seemed, could boast nothing to compare with the quality of the objects found at the villa of El Ruedo (Almedinilla), which include a number of sculptures relating to Greco-Roman mythology and to local religious cults and, in particular, the magnificent bronze figures of Hermaphrodite and Hypnos (or Somnus).

As early as the 1950s there had been one particularly significant discovery from the Roman period in the centre of the modern town of Priego, in Calle Carrera de las Monjas, consisting of some thirty terracotta busts of female figures, together with others representing Bacchus and Minerva. These figures, dating from the second century AD, are most likely to be related to a funeral rite, probably cremation. There had also been a small number of finds made in other parts of the central urban area, dating from the Roman period and including several fragments of pottery, tiles, a bronze coin minted in Mérida in the first half of the first century AD, a silver bracelet and a fragment of a Corinthian capital. Archaeologists believed that a systematic investigation could well produce evidence of a more important settlement during the Roman period. Then, in the year 2000, evidence was found during the excavation of an Islamic necropolis, below the square now known as El Palenque, of a grave of Roman origin. In the years which followed, the sites of more Roman graves and cremations were discovered in the urban area, and also a number of ceramic ovens, including two in the westernmost part of the modern town, in what is now the district of Los Almendros. Perhaps these actually belonged to the *municipium* of Ipolcobulcoba (now Carcabuey). Other finds included a Roman coin from the fourth century AD. By 2007, clear proof had emerged of the existence of a Roman villa, which had stood close to the site of the earlier major discovery, in the area around what is now the Calle Carrera de las Monjas and near to the present-day town hall. This villa had occupied a commanding position, dominating the countryside below, with an ample water supply but well away from the marshy land around the area now corresponding to the Fuente del Rey. It dates from between the middle of the first century AD and the middle of the second century and was built of local travertine limestone. It consisted of two separate elements: one forming the living accommodation, which included a dining room with a mosaic floor and baths, and the other, about 150 metres away, the farm buildings. In addition, archaeologists now began work on the exploration, beneath part of the present-day Calle Ramón y Cajal, of a Hispano-Roman necropolis, with a lime kiln and several graves. It was probably here that the remains of the villa's owners and their families were interred.

The existence of the settlement in Priego offers a possible explanation of the name which the later Islamic town was to acquire. The village would have been known in Latin as a *vicus*, and the rural area in which it was set would have been termed a *pagus*. A *pagus* was a territory of minor importance dependant on a larger one, in this case probably the municipal area of Ipolcobulcoba. It seems likely that the villa corresponded to the estate (both agricultural and residential) of a landowner from this nearby town.[11] It is logical enough, therefore, to argue that the Arabised name Bāguh is formed from the Latin term *pagus*, whose pronunciation was probably very similar. Indeed, this continuity in the use of the name would appear to imply that the settlement of Roman origin remained in existence until early in the eighth century when the arrival of Islamic troops led to the foundation of what was to become the Muslim town of madīnat Bāguh.

---

[11] Carmona, 2016, 240.

BEGINNINGS

*

As part of a series of migrations by Germanic tribes, the Visigoths entered the Iberian Peninsula en masse in the early sixth century, dominating it politically for 200 years. Nominally, they united the Peninsula under a single ruler, but in practice their influence on the lives of most of its people was minimal. The pattern of habitation in the Priego area seems to have remained more or less unchanged, with the settlements from the Roman period continuing to exist but with very few cases of the establishment of new communities. Archaeological finds relating to the Visigothic period include pottery (notably late *sigillata*), bronze items such as buckles, some Germanic in style, and notably a pair of weights with inscriptions in Greek. These are an indication of Byzantine trading links. In the mid-sixth century, a province of the Byzantine Empire was established in the south-east of the Peninsula. There is no suggestion, however, of the Priego area coming under its direct influence or control.

The most significant discovery from this period, however, has been on the *cortijo* (farmstead) of El Arrimadizo, some 10 kilometres south-west of Priego: a Christian burial area, dating from the late seventh or early eighth century and possibly associated with a small religious community.

In most respects, information about Priego during the Visigothic period is very scarce, and there is no evidence at all to suggest any significant social or economic progress over the two centuries of Visigothic dominance. This absence of development is in marked contrast with the evolution during this time of nearby communities: Ipolcobulcoba, where a Christian basilica was established, and especially Egabrum (now Cabra), situated some 20 kilometres to the west of the modern town of Priego, which under the Visigoths became the seat of a bishopric and an important political, administrative and economic centre. But all of this was to change with the Islamic conquest of the Iberian Peninsula.

Madīnat Bāguh: Priego de Córdoba during the Islamic period

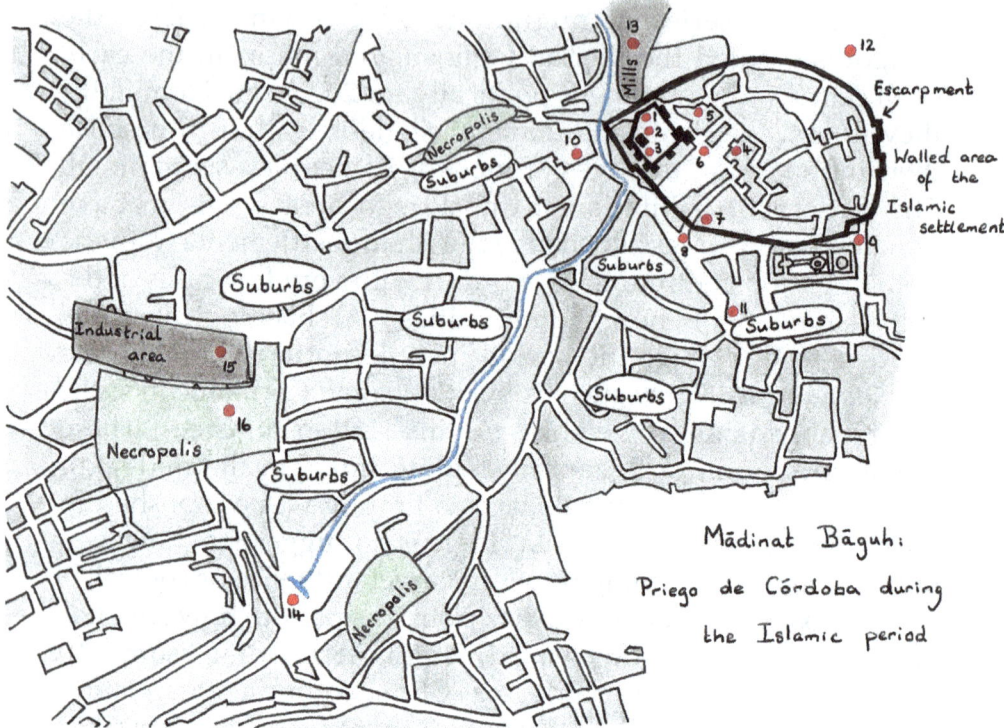

1. Alcazaba: castle
2. Torre del Homenaje: literally 'tribute tower' but equivalent to castle keep
3. Aljibe: water tank, inside the castle walls
4. Main mosque: on the site of the present-day church of La Asunción
5. Probable location of a further mosque: on the site of the church of Santiago, now disappeared
6. Aljibe: water tank, outside the castle walls
7. Public baths
8. Gateway: subsequently known as Puerta de Santa Ana
9. Gateway: Puerta del Sol
10. Possible site of another mosque, on the site of the present-day church of San Pedro
11. Possible site of another mosque, on the site of the present-day church of La Aurora
12. La Cubé: a naturally formed platform below the town, on the banks of the River Salado, with evidence of agricultural terracing
13. Area of mills
14. Spring: the source of the river which, now canalised, runs beneath the present-day Calle Río
15. Industrial area: evidence of craft and pottery workshops, in the region of the present-day Calle San Marcos
16. Necropolis situated on the site of the modern-day square of El Palenque

CHAPTER 2

Madīnat Bāguh

In the course of the second decade of the eighth century AD, the Iberian Peninsula was overrun by Muslim invaders, part of a long process of expansion which had begun some eighty years previously. The overthrow of the already weak Visigothic monarchy and invasion of its Iberian kingdom by Islamic forces in 711 was followed by a period of rapid consolidation, during which Islamic control was extended throughout almost all of the Peninsula. The Muslim commander, Tāriq ibn Ziyād, as one of his first acts, dispatched troops northwards from the south coast to Córdoba, which succumbed after a brief period of resistance, and before the end of the year, Toledo, the Visigothic capital, also surrendered. Forty-five years later, the Umayyad 'Abd al-Raḥmān I established himself in Córdoba at the head of a dynasty which was to rule al-Andalus (the name that the Muslims gave to the old Roman province of Hispania) until 1031.[12] Within al-Andalus, Priego, which came to be known in Arabic as madīnat Bāguh, was to achieve prominence as the centre of an administrative district. From the time of the conquest, over six centuries were to pass before, on being definitively conquered by Alfonso XI in 1341, the town finally became incorporated into the Christian kingdom of Castile. Thus, Priego de Córdoba effectively owes its existence to its role in Islamic Spain.

There is no evidence to indicate whether the town established by the Muslims was a continuation of the previously existing

---

[12] The Umayyads were the first Muslim ruling dynasty, established in Damascus in 661 AD. In 750 AD, they were driven out by the 'Abbāsids, but subsequently under 'Abd al-Rahmān I, they achieved dominance in al-Andalus.

settlement of Roman origin or whether it was effectively a new foundation. However, it is certainly possible that the Islamic newcomers who first occupied the area which was to become Priego or Bāguh will have found there a small rural community, in all likelihood Christian. There is, as we have seen, evidence (notably the burial ground at El Arrimadizo) to point to the Christianisation of the area during the Visigothic period. Provided that it had submitted readily to the Muslim invaders, such a community would have been easily absorbed into Islamic society, either by conversion or, if the Christians chose to retain their religion, through the payment of a special tax and the acceptance of a number of strict constraints.

It is likely that the distribution of land among its new masters now took place on a tribal basis. The invading forces were made up of a mixture of Arabs and Berbers of North African origin. There is a dearth of information with regard to the process by which the territory of al-Andalus was shared out during the early years of the conquest, but it is probable that the Priego area, if settled at an early stage, was occupied principally by Arabs rather than Berbers.

The point at which the area was first inhabited by Muslims is still open to debate. Within two years of the initial conquest of the Peninsula in 711, there was certainly an important Arab presence in Qal'at Astalīr (now Alcalá la Real, some 25 kilometres to the east of Bāguh), and to the north and west, Muslim communities were soon settled in what are now the towns of Baena, Lucena and Cabra. In the case of Bāguh, however, we do not know the date of the first Islamic settlement. Perhaps the travertine limestone platform on which the core of the Muslim town would eventually be situated was simply too wet and marshy to encourage habitation.[13] On the other hand, the outlying areas, accessible and with a ready water supply, so important for agriculture and so fundamental to Islamic culture, must have seemed a much more attractive proposition.

---

[13] This would explain why the Roman villa was situated 200 metres to the west of the travertine platform. See Cano Montoro, 2015, 24.

The fourteenth-century Arab scholar Ibn al-Jatīb records the presence in the year 745 of Syrian troops in what appears to be 'Bago' and has been taken by some scholars to be Bāguh. This reading is disputed but it does seem possible that in the mid-eighth century, Syrian forces, which had arrived as reinforcements following a Berber uprising against the Arab elite, were present in this area.[14]

The first indisputable reference to madīnat Bāguh does not in fact come until the second half of the ninth century, although it is clear that by this point the town had already acquired quite considerable political and military importance. In 863, Muḥammad I, the first independent emir of al-Andalus, dispatched a military expedition on a punitive raid (*sā'ifah*, in Spanish, *aceifa*) directed at the northern Christian kingdom of Asturias-León. This is the first such expedition for which we have detailed information and significantly the district of Bāguh figures as contributing a force of 900 horsemen. It is listed as a *kūra* or *cora*, a territorial and administrative area based on a town or city (or *madīna*) of the same name. By this point, then, madīnat Bāguh had already achieved the status equivalent to that of a provincial capital, and it would have been governed by a *qa'id* or military commander and would have possessed a substantial garrison. The size of the force that Bāguh provided, although far below the largest contributor, Medina Sidonia (6,000), was well above the lowest included in the list, the present-day Reina in Badajoz (106), and this suggests that the area had quite a prominent military role. The figure of 900 horsemen would clearly not have been as great as the total number of troops available, and so the size of the contribution seems to imply quite a high density of population in the area.

The archaeological evidence indicates that the initial Islamic settlement in what was to become madīnat Bāguh was in the

---

[14] See, for example, Carmona Ávila, 2009, 161 and 174, note 1, and Cano Montoro, 2015, 12–15. Cano Montoro cites evidence, both textual and archaeological (hoards of silver coins), which suggests an Islamic presence in the Priego area by the middle of the eighth century.

district corresponding to the present-day Barrio de la Villa, situated towards the eastern edge of the modern town. Its natural boundaries, notably the *Tajo* or escarpment to the east, imposed tight limitations on its growth, and to the west, the core of the town with its castle and mosques was protected by a ditch and a wall. The industrial and residential districts that developed in the area stretching away to the west had no fortifications.[15]

In the first instance, it is likely that the settlement that was to become madīnat Bāguh owed its origin to the need for an administrative centre – probably for the purpose of taxation – between the existing towns of Qal'at Astalīr (Alcalá la Real) and Egabrum (Cabra). Any indigenous population would have continued to live and work in the community, subject to the taxes imposed on non-Muslims, and with conversions taking place progressively for socioeconomic reasons. The organisation of the Islamic community was essentially tribal. It is likely that the settlement that was established in the area of the Barrio de la Villa, probably by the late eighth century but possibly later, steadily acquired the characteristics of a *madīna*, until it eventually took on the role of a *kūra*.[16] The use of this term *kūra* implies that by the time of the *aceifa* in the 860s, madīnat Bāguh was the administrative centre of an agricultural area, and we can imagine that, as this role developed, its increased importance will naturally have led to its significant military role.

The works of Muslim scholars over the following centuries give us a picture of the characteristics that led to the area's growing prestige and prosperity. They emphasise the richness of the land for the production of cereal crops, grapes and also saffron of excellent quality, and repeatedly they dwell on the qualities of the water: near to the town of madīnat Bāguh, we are

---

[15] See Carmona Ávila, 2009, 234.

[16] Cano Montoro, 2015, 38, suggests that the creation of the administrative area of Bāguh is associated with a process of reorganisation that took place in second half of the eighth century.

told by the eleventh-century geographer al-'Uḍhrī, there is a spring whose water can dissolve kidney stones. Writing in the tenth century, the Arab geographer al-Muqaddasī (or al-Maqdisi) cites a native of Córdoba as informing him that Bāguh, one of Córdoba's thirteen districts, apart from having rivers that provided water to drive mills, possessed an abundance of mulberry, olive and fig trees. Of the importance of the first two of these, much more will be heard at a later stage in Priego's history. The twelfth-century scholar al-Idrīsī writes of madīnat Bāguh that, although it is of small size, it is extremely attractive on account of the amount of water that flows across its territory. The rivers drive a number of water mills within the town itself, and its land, covered with vines, orchards and vegetable gardens, could not be more fertile. We hear from another source that the wines of the area were highly celebrated.

We know nothing of developments in madīnat Bāguh over the two decades which followed the expedition of 863, but this absence of comment in itself suggests that this was a time of peace in the area. In the year 886, however, Bāguh became involved in a highly significant popular rebellion against the supremacy of the emirate in Córdoba. The rule of Muhammad I (852–86) had been characterised by a climate of revolt, and the most conspicuous example of this was the uprising led by 'Umar ibn Ḥafṣūn, which began in 886 in the district of Rayya (now Málaga) and lasted for some forty years. 'Umar may well have been of Visigothic descent. He promised independence from the central control of Córdoba and freedom from the heavy tax burden that it imposed. So great was his success that at one point his forces reached the outskirts of Córdoba and threatened to overturn the emirate. It was only under the rule of the powerful 'Abd al-Raḥmān III (912–61) that the insurrection headed by 'Umar ibn Ḥafṣūn and his sons would be finally overcome and that this period of *fitna* or civil war would be brought to an end.

At an early point in the uprising, while the new emir, al-Mhundir, son of Muḥammad I, had yet to be installed in Córdoba, the rebel forces made their way northwards, captured madīnat Bāguh and imprisoned its governor. We are told that they seized valuable booty. In the following year, troops sent from Córdoba retook the town and another rebel army was subsequently defeated nearby. 'Umar ibn Ḥafṣūn, however, while feigning submission to the emir, laid siege to Qal'at Astalīr and, overcoming another army sent from Córdoba, seized both Qal'at Astalīr and madīnat Bāguh. From 889, 'Umar's relative and adviser, Sa'īd ibn Walid ibn Mastana, set himself up as a virtually independent governor of Bāguh and nearby Lukk (Luque), and the town was in rebel hands until 894 when an Umayyad army recaptured it, laying waste the surrounding area. The historian Ibn Ḥayyān comments on the devastation caused to the town of Bāguh by these conflicts. There remained considerable resistance in the *kūra* and it took almost another thirty years for this to be overcome, with a number of key strongholds being surrendered in the years 921–22. The area was remote enough from Córdoba and the surrounding terrain difficult enough to enable Mastana and his descendants (the Banū Mastana) to carry on their struggle against the Umayyads with relative impunity. During this period, Bāguh changed hands between the rebel forces and those of the emir on at least four occasions. Near madīnat Bāguh there were several strategically situated *hisn*, fortifications controlling the surrounding area and points of access. Two castles in particular are mentioned in Islamic sources as being captured towards the end of the campaign against the rebels: Ribarăs (possibly the present-day village of Sileras, situated 12 kilometres north-east of Priego but now considered more likely to correspond to Sierra Leones, situated about 4 kilometres north of Priego where the rivers Salado and Zagrilla meet); and also 'Āliya (previously identified with Torre Alta but more recently with Alhucemas, in the mountainous area of the Sierra Horconera, south-west of Priego).[17]

It seems that at some point following this period of conflict

---

[17] For the identification of these two castles, see Carmona Ávila, 2010, 148–50.

Bāguh ceased to be the centre of an independent *kūra* and was integrated into the larger administrative area known as Kūra Ilbīra or Elvira. We do know that in 929 a new governor, Ahmad ibn Qāsim al-Kalbī, was appointed to Bāguh, an indication that at this point it had recovered its independent status, and a succession of new appointments to this post were made in the following years. Archaeological evidence reinforces the sense of the area's military importance during this period. However, by 974, Bāguh was once again being listed as a territory of Elvira, a position that it was to continue to occupy until the fall of the Cordoban caliphate at the beginning of the following century.

For some fifty years, Muslim Spain was dominated by the figure of 'Abd al-Raḥmān III, who in 929 assumed the title of Caliph and a surname which meant 'Protector of the Religion of God'. The implication of this was that he claimed full independence from the Abbāsid caliph in the east and became the first Umayyad caliph of al-Andalus. Córdoba became a political centre of great power and brilliance, and its prestige was exemplified by such projects as the construction of the great palace – indeed a town in its own right – of madīnat al-Zahrā. The reign of 'Abd al-Raḥmān III was a period characterised by rich and varied cultural achievement, of military dominance over the Christian kingdoms of the north of the Peninsula, and also of flourishing trade and efficient administration and tax-collecting. In many respects, this splendour continued during the fifteen-year rule of 'Abd al-Raḥmān's son and successor, al-Ḥakam II. A provincial town such as madīnat Bāguh will no doubt have benefitted greatly throughout this lengthy period from the political stability and the prosperity that it brought, though we must be careful about assuming that the cultural glories of the Umayyad capital were widely reflected in al-Andalus.

When al-Ḥakam died in 976, leaving a twelve-year-old son, Hishām II, to inherit the caliphate, it was Ibn Abī 'Āmir, better known as al-Manṣūr, who came to dominance and who went on to govern autocratically until he died in 1002. A fearsome military commander, he was famed for his devastating raids on the Christian north, partly, at least, intended as a demonstration of his power to the people of al-Andalus. The level of conscription was high and the rate of taxation increased. The effects of this were undoubtedly felt by the people of Bāguh, but the political situation remained more or less stable until the death of al-Manṣūr's son 'Abd al-Malik al-Muẓaffar in 1008. What followed, however, was effectively a period of twenty years of civil war as different factions sought to assert their authority. By 1031, the Umayyad caliphate had been dissolved and the city of Córdoba had entirely lost its position of dominance and authority over a fragmented al-Andalus, which broke down into several independent political units, known as the *taifa* kingdoms.

At some point during this period of conflict, Bāguh came to form part of the territories controlled by a branch of the Zīrid dynasty (of North African Berber origin) which in 1013 established a *taifa* kingdom with its capital in madīnat Gharnāṭah (Medina Garnata), the present-day city of Granada. Bāguh was now under the authority of a governor subject to the sultan of Granada. Islamic sources provide us with little information about the development of Bāguh during this period, although there are occasional glimpses of events which reflect the continuing importance of the town. One such episode occurred in 1073, when King Alfonso VI (ruler of the Christian kingdom of Castile-León) dispatched his ambassador Pedro Ansúrez to Granada to collect tribute and this was refused by its seventeen-year-old Zīrid sultan. The ruler of the kingdom of Sevilla, al-Mu'tamid ibn 'Abbād, sent his visir Ibn-'Ammār to negotiate a treaty by which the kingdom of Sevilla would form an alliance with the Christians, leading to the conquest of Granada, the immediate result of which was that Granada was obliged to pay the tribute demanded by Alfonso. It was at madīnat Bāguh that the negotiations between Pedro Ansúrez and Ibn-'Ammār took place.

The Zīrid dynasty in Granada was overthrown in 1090 by the

first of two waves of invaders of Berber origin from Africa – the Almoravids – who progressively seized control of the *taifa* kingdoms of al-Andalus, and Bāguh seems to have fallen into their hands without resistance. Again, historical sources contain very little information about events there over this period – except an indication that madīnat Bāguh may well have been one of the towns attacked during a raid by Castilian forces in the year 1126. Similarly, Islamic writers have very little to tell us about the history of madīnat Bāguh under the Almohad dynasty, whose forces entered the Peninsula in 1147 and by 1172 had extended their control to all of Muslim Iberia. The geographer al-Idrīsī, writing in the mid-twelfth century, tells us that madīnat Bāguh continued to belong to the district of Elvira and that it was one of its principal towns along with Loja and Guadix. Al-Idrīsī also, as we have already seen, sings the praises of madīnat Bāguh as the centre of a rich agricultural area.[18] The Christian chronicles include some telling details in their account of the town's capture by Fernando III in 1225, which indicate the extent to which it had flourished over the previous century: we know, for example, that by this point Almohad knights 'of illustrious birth' and clearly of considerable wealth were resident there. In addition, we have tangible evidence of the prestige acquired by madīnat Bāguh during the period of Almohad dominance. This includes the discovery in the urban area of an outstandingly rich treasure, consisting of some 8,500 silver coins, and there is evidence, too, that coins were minted in the town. We also know, for example, that the children of an individual high in the Almohad hierarchy were present in the town and that a noted scholar was commanded to move there from Granada to act as their tutor. It was, moreover, particularly significant that Berbers of the Masmuda tribe, an influential force in the Almohad religious movement, settled in the area of madīnat Bāguh.[19]

---

[18] Peláez del Rosal and Rivas Carmona, 96.

[19] For a discussion of the evidence for the prestige acquired by Bāguh under the Almohads, see Carmona, 2009, 234–35.

Nevertheless, it is not until the occasion of that initial reconquest by Castilian forces that we have any further firm documentary evidence about the details of the town's history.

*

If information from written sources over this lengthy period is scant, archaeological evidence, with finds dating mainly from the tenth to the thirteenth century, is much more extensive. The nucleus of the town or *madīna* was a walled area which broadly corresponded to the district occupying the north-eastern corner of the modern town, known as the Barrio de la Villa. It has been calculated that its population will have been between 600 and 1,400 people, although this figure was significantly increased by those living in the outlying parts of the town. The walled area was some distance away from the old Roman settlement and was separated from it by the river. This flowed down from the spring whose position is marked by the present-day Fuente del Rey. The side of the town least well defended by its walls was afforded some protection by the river, which in later centuries was channelled underground; indeed, with the exception of the old walled town, most of the travertine platform on which Priego stands was a marshy area in need of artificial drainage. To the north and east, the 'Tajo' or escarpment, forming a natural defence some 30 metres in height, was reinforced with worked stone and constituted an important part of the town's fortifications. The al-Qasar or *alcazaba*, corresponding to the present castle (which would be completely rebuilt after the town's eventual recapture in the fourteenth century by the Christian forces), was situated at the western end of the walled area. The original town walls, probably seriously damaged during the period of conflict during the late ninth and early tenth centuries, were replaced under the Caliphate and the perimeter was thus extended further towards the south-west; and the *alcazaba* (which had previously projected out beyond the walls) was brought inside the enclosed area. Into the walls were set heavily protected gateways, notably, opening to the south, that which is now known as the Puerta de Santa Ana, the most important entry to the fortified area; and to the south-east the Puerta del Sol, with its octagonal tower. With the much-increased threat of attack by Christian forces from the late twelfth century, the walls were strengthened and a number of towers added.

The present-day Barrio de la Villa continues to reflect the typical structure of an Islamic town, similar, if on a much smaller scale, to the Jewish quarter in Córdoba and the Barrio de Santa Cruz in Seville. The streets are narrow, some less than a metre in width, winding and labyrinthine, with large blocks of housing and numerous small squares.

Within the walled area there was an extensive set of public baths, situated in the area of the Puerta de Santa Ana, in addition to the baths for private use within the *alcazaba*. A large well and water deposits (*aljibes*), dating from the Almohad period, were situated both inside and outside the walls of the *alcazaba*.

There is at present no firm evidence with regard to the location of the town's mosques, but it is considered highly likely that one of them (probably the *aljama* or principal mosque of the community) stood on the site of the present-day church of La Asunción, in the area of the *alcazaba*. Another is believed to have occupied the position of what was subsequently the church of Santiago (now disappeared), situated in the centre of the Barrio de la Villa. In addition, later references suggest that there were mosques outside the town walls where the churches of La Aurora and San Pedro now stand.

The archaeological evidence makes it clear that the town developed gradually, starting with the core of the Barrio de la Villa, centred around its mosque. This was followed by the area partly given over to agriculture, further to the south and east, which later came to be known as the Barrio de la Morería; and finally the part of the town which lay outside the walls. Here, extending towards the west, there was an area occupied by craftsmen. There is evidence of the existence of forges and of a number of potters' workshops (for example, in the area corresponding to the present-day Calle San Marcos): a large variety of pottery has been discovered and also a kiln dating from the Almohad period. There are also clear indications that, separated by the river from the walled area of madīnat Bāguh, extensive outlying districts, stretching as far as the present-day square of El Palenque, included domestic housing, agricultural storage areas and – on the outskirts – at least three necropoleis or cemeteries. In areas such as La Cubé, below the town on the banks of the river Salado, there was early agricultural terracing. It was during the Islamic period, too, that the first steps were taken to channel and reroute the water flowing down from the spring situated to the south-west of the town walls.

It was, as we have seen, during the period of Almohad domination (beginning in the mid-twelfth century) that madīnat Bāguh achieved the height of its prosperity, serving as an important commercial centre for the surrounding area. Habitation of the area will have taken various forms. Some of the outlying settlements, mostly dating from earlier, less peaceful times, stood on high ground, as in the case of Peñas Doblas or Los Almogávares in the Sierra de Albayate (near Almedinilla). In addition, there are clear indications during the Islamic period of habitation in caves, notably in the Cueva de los Mármoles and Huerta Anguita (Las Angosturas). El Jardín del Moro, on the other hand, situated in the foothills of the mountainous area of La Horconera, is the best example of a fortified settlement, with a substantial stretch of wall and a well and water deposit sunk into the rock. There is evidence, too, however, both archaeological and textual, of the existence of several settlements with no signs of fortification, located in low-lying areas. Some of these appear to represent the origin of present-day villages which lie within the municipal area of Priego, such as Zagrilla Alta, Castil de Campos and Las Lagunillas.

A further feature of the landscape of the area around madīnat Bāguh, still much in evidence today, has been the presence of cylindrical watchtowers or *atalayas*. It is estimated that there were about fifteen of these altogether: built on commanding heights and forming a network of inter-communicating observation posts, they constituted a fundamental part of the town's defences. It is argued that the construction of most of these towers dates from the period in the thirteenth and fourteenth centuries when Priego was part of the frontier area. Almost all of them show evidence of Islamic building techniques. Some scholars associate their construction with the period between 1327 and 1341 when Priego was in Muslim hands for a second time, but it is also possible that some of them go back to an earlier stage in the town's Islamic history.[20]

It is unfortunate that we possess so little concrete information about the events which make up the history of madīnat Bāguh, but that evidence which has come down to us leaves no doubt that under the Almohads it enjoyed both prosperity and prestige. At this point, however, we must turn to look at the events, beginning in the early decades of the thirteenth century, which saw Priego transformed from a flourishing Islamic town into a bulwark of Christian Spain.

The Adarve
This view of Priego, taken from the east, illustrates clearly why the town played such an important role as a military centre. The *Tajo* or escarpment forms a formidable natural defence which in the Middle Ages and beyond was supplemented by a ring of fortifications. The natural balcony on its edge is known as the *Adarve*, and behind it is the Barrio de la Villa, which corresponds to the town's original urban nucleus. The mountain peak in the background is La Tiñosa. *Photograph by Antonio Jesús Villena.*

---

[20] See Carmona Ávila, Luna Osuna and Moreno Rosa, 2002, 149.

CHAPTER 3

Christendom Victorious

It is not really appropriate to talk of the Christian 'reconquest' of Priego in the thirteenth century, as there is no firm evidence that there ever had been a Christian town on this site before the establishment of madīnat Bāguh. Nevertheless, the capture of the Islamic town in 1225 has to be seen within the context of the centuries-long process by which the Christian kingdoms progressively took control of the whole of the Iberian Peninsula. We have seen how the break-up of the Umayyad caliphate at the beginning of the eleventh century marked a crucial turning point and left the so-called *taifa* kingdoms vulnerable to financial exploitation and ultimately conquest. What ensued, however, was far from a one-way process, and the arrival in the Peninsula of first the Almoravids and later the Almohads allowed Islamic communities like madīnat Bāguh to enjoy extended periods of relative peace and prosperity. This was particularly the case in the late twelfth century, and as late as 1195 the Almohads' overwhelming victory over the Christian army at Alarcos reinforced their dominance.

By the second decade of the thirteenth century, however, the situation had again changed. With the enthusiastic support of the Church, Alfonso VIII of Castile was beginning to encroach on Muslim territory and raids were launched as far south as the city of Jaén, some 55 kilometres north-east of madīnat Bāguh. In July 1212, the Christian forces, led by Alfonso, did battle with a large army on the plain of Las Navas de Tolosa, just south of the Despeñaperros pass through the Sierra Morena mountains, one of the principal routes into the south of the Peninsula. The overwhelming Christian victory left the Islamic communities of

Andalucía permanently open to attack from the north. Although the towns of Baeza and Úbeda were captured and destroyed almost immediately, plague in the Christian army prevented it for the time being from pursuing its campaign further south, and further problems, including a period of famine and then internal conflict following Alfonso's death, gave the vulnerable Muslim towns a further period of respite. It was not until some twelve years after the battle of Las Navas de Tolosa that Fernando III, Alfonso's grandson and successor as king of Castile, was in a strong enough position to continue the push southwards.

Setting off through the Despeñaperros pass with a vast army, which included troops provided by the noblemen of his kingdom, the city militias and the military Orders, he gained further support by means of an alliance with 'Abd Alāh al-Bayyāsī, the independent emir of Baeza who went on to take control of an area extending as far as Córdoba and Sevilla. The Christian forces besieged the heavily fortified and strongly defended city of Jaén, but without adequate siege engines they were unable to capture it. They then turned towards the south-west, sparing the town of Alcaudete at al-Bayyāsī's request, but instead moving to attack madīnat Bāguh. This was probably in July 1225, though, curiously, there is inconsistency among sources with regard to the year. What is not in doubt is the importance of the capture of the town. The Christian chronicles emphasise its wealth and prosperity, and it clearly represented an attractive prize. The assault began after a break of two days, during which the Christian army devastated the surrounding area, and in the course of the attack the great majority of the town's inhabitants were slaughtered. The only survivors were those who took refuge in the town's castle: with al-Bayyāsī as an intermediary, they negotiated with the Christian monarch an agreement which gave them safety in return for the rendition of the castle and the payment of the huge sum of 80,000 silver *maravedís*. The hostages that were handed over included fifty-five Muslim ladies of noble rank (who were placed under the authority of al-Bayyāsī), fifty knights and 900 other Moors. The fortress was razed to the ground. Madīnat Bāguh had been the first town to be captured during this campaign and its brutal treatment will undoubtedly have been intended to be seen as exemplary, a lesson to other Muslim towns and cities that immediate surrender would be their best option. The fact that in the seventeenth century Fernando III was to be made a saint does not in any way suggest that he was less given to hideous acts of cruelty towards his enemies than any other medieval monarch.

In due course, the Christian army moved on southwards towards Loja and the *vega* (the flood plain) in the approaches to Granada. According to the chronicle of the Order of Calatrava, troops were left in madīnat Bāguh with suitable provisions for the defence of the castle, although there is an apparent contradiction here with what we are told elsewhere about the total destruction of the town's fortifications. Another twelve years were to pass before Fernando was to capture the far bigger prize of the city of Córdoba itself, and it is not until 1245 that we have any more firm information about the history of the town known to the Christians as Priego. It is likely that in the months that followed the original capture, Fernando III's army had returned there temporarily, having devastated the land further south, but that within a few months the area fell once again into Muslim hands. Possibly it had been handed over by Fernando to al-Bayyāsī, on whose death in 1226 it was seized by the Almohads.[21] We know that a year later the towns of Andújar, Martos and Baeza (some way further north) marked the southern limit of the territory then controlled by the Christians, and it appears that Priego had by now been repopulated by Muslims.

Following the capture of Córdoba in 1236, however, King Fernando continued the process of establishing firm control over the conquered territories, and in 1240–41 he was again

---

[21] For this suggestion, see Carmona Ávila, Lunes Osuna and Moreno Rosa, 152.

campaigning in the area of the Subbética, capturing a number of castles. In February 1245, he donated to the diocese of Córdoba the town and castle of Tiñosa, situated 10 kilometres from Priego. Later in the same year, he launched an attack on the areas around Jaén, Alcaudete and Alcalá de Benzaide (known to the Muslims as Qal'at Astalīr and nowadays called Alcalá la Real). In the course of the siege of Jaén, King Fernando promised the towns of Alcaudete and Priego to the military Order of Calatrava, and in March 1246, when Jaén was finally captured, Priego again fell into Christian hands and came under the jurisdiction of the Order. It was the Order of Calatrava which was to be responsible for the rebuilding of Priego's castle and other fortifications and for its defence against further Muslim attack.

The first military Orders, such as those of the Temple and of the Hospitallers of Saint John, had come into existence in the course of the Crusades, but they rapidly extended their activities into the Iberian Peninsula where a number of national Orders (most notably Alcántara, Calatrava and Santiago) were established. In the twelfth century, the Orders, embodying an ideal which fused Christian zeal and knightly prowess, played a vital part in resisting the thrust of the invading Almohad forces. The Order of Calatrava, founded in 1158, went on to achieve immense military and political power, possessing numerous castles in frontier regions and exercising feudal authority over its vassals. In 1246, Fernando ceded Priego to Calatrava and it became an *encomienda* of the Order, under the lordship of the *comendador*, the knight assigned to it.[22] He in turn was responsible to the bishop of Jaén. Priego was one of ten towns held by the Order within the diocese, and following an agreement reached in 1256, the Order of Calatrava was to have the right to all the tithes paid by these towns to the bishop, such as those corresponding to oil, livestock, wool and cheese. The brothers of the Order would not be liable to pay any taxes to the bishop, and their vassals would pay one third of the amount due

---

[22] *Encomienda* is a feudal term, derived from the verb meaning 'to entrust'.

to the bishop and two thirds to the *comendador* (though in the case of Muslims the whole amount was payable to the *comendador*). In addition, the Order, rather than the bishop, had the right to donations and legacies, which previously would have gone to the diocese.

It is from this period that there survives, in the cave of Cholones, near to the village of Zagrilla Alta, the representation, drawn in charcoal, of a warrior-monk of the Order of Calatrava, clad in a long tunic and wearing a hemispherical helmet, with his arms raised and looking towards a cross of his Order.

Priego was a frontier town. Twenty-five kilometres away, Qal'at Astalīr (or Alcalá de Benzaide) would remain in Muslim hands until 1341. Given the inherent dangers, it was difficult to repopulate the area. It is known that the town of Priego had received its *fuero* or charter before 1253, and a town council existed by 1288 when there is a record of King Sancho IV conceding to the town's citizens exemption from the *portazgo* or toll. There is also evidence of a long-standing dispute over rights and duties with nearby Tiñosa, an enclave in the Order's territory which belonged to the diocese of Córdoba, but in 1281 Tiñosa was incorporated into the *encomienda* of Priego. By this point, the castle of Tiñosa with its water tank had been destroyed on the king's orders. Its upkeep had proved too difficult and expensive as a result of constant Muslim attacks, and so its demolition was ordered in order to prevent it being of use to the Islamic forces. Tiñosa's fate illustrates clearly the constant threat which faced Priego, just 10 kilometres away.

The military Orders rapidly acquired a significant political role and in the early 1280s the Order of Calatrava – and Priego in particular – was involved in the conflict which developed between Alfonso X and his son and successor, Sancho IV. In 1282, it was the scene of a meeting between Sancho and Muḥammad II of Granada at which the Muslim king pledged the Castilian prince his support in return for the handing over of the castle of Arenas. Six years later, King Sancho was to reward the town of Priego with the grant of privileges and tax exemptions.

The reorganisation of Priego's territory appears to have been based on the divisions established by the Muslims. There can be no doubt that the Christian town was smaller than the prosperous Islamic community that it replaced. We do know, however, that its defensive system was reinforced and the perimeter wall strengthened. The Muslim castle or *alcazaba* was rebuilt with its imposing main tower (*torre del homenaje*, literally 'homage tower'). The old Muslim suburbs, impossible to defend, were abandoned, as were the cultivated areas outside the walls, such as La Cubé. The rich and varied agriculture associated with madīnat Bāguh was no longer possible in an area that suffered frequent raids, and the farming of livestock, easier to protect behind the fortifications, almost certainly became predominant.

Priego, no doubt on account of the strength of its defences, continued to be held by the Order of Calatrava in spite of the continuing Muslim incursions. These attacks led to the fall of the castles of Alcaudete and Castillo de Locubín in 1300, which left Priego cut off from the important centre of the Order at Martos, some 35 kilometres to the north-east. It is known that in 1319 the body of Sancho IV's brother Prince Pedro, killed during a raid into the kingdom of Granada, was first taken to Priego before its eventual burial in Burgos. And it was probably eight years after this, during a period of division and conflict within the Order, that Priego again fell into Muslim hands. The *Chronicle of Alfonso XI* tells that this was brought about through the treachery of a squire left in charge of the town by its *comendador*, don Pedro Ruiz de Córdoba, and that Muḥammad IV of Granada had promised the squire payment and marriage to a lady of his royal household.[23] The chronicle does not confirm whether or not the treacherous individual received his reward. It is not uncommon in medieval chronicles for military defeats to be blamed on treachery or the misconduct of a hapless individual, however, and Muslim sources give a very different account of how Priego

---

[23] For this account, see Peláez del Rosal and Quintanilla Raso, 71–72.

fell, attributing a vital role to the Granadan minister (or *ḥāyib*) Riḍwān:

> *Ḥāyib* Riḍwān and his army launched a raid on the 26th of the first month of the year 733 [1332 AD] against madīnat Bāguh, a town famous for the abundance of its waters and its fertile lands. He seized the surrounding area, imposing a severe siege, and prevented the arrival of assistance. He took the town by means of a direct assault and subsequently repopulated it with defenders, consolidating it with *morabitos*.[24]

Morabitos were the soldier monks entrusted with the defence of frontiers, and the related term *rábita* was applied to fortified convents situated in key military areas.

Whichever version we accept, by 1332, Priego was part of the Nasrid kingdom of Granada.[25] The frontier between Muslim territory and the Christian lands to the north and west probably ran along the river Salado. It is possible that the watchtowers or *atalayas* mentioned in the previous chapter date from this period and their function may have been that of *rábitas*.[26] Madīnat Bāguh served as an important base for raiding Islamic forces, and the *Chronicle of Alfonso XI* documents, for example, a Christian attack on a Muslim mule train bringing it supplies.[27]

*

Alfonso XI of Castile and León was the grandson of Sancho IV and succeeded to the throne when he was just one year old. His minority was marked by political conflict but when he came of age he set about achieving the dual objectives of imposing firm

---

[24] Arjona Castro, 143.

[25] This was the last Muslim dynasty in the Iberian Peninsula and ruled the Emirate of Granada from 1230 until it fell into Christian hands in 1492.

[26] Arjona Castro, 144–46.

[27] Peláez del Rosal and Quintanilla Raso, 72–73.

control over the conflictive nobles of his kingdom and overcoming the Nasrid kingdom, the last bastion of Islamic power in the Peninsula. He was to die as a victim of the Black Death in 1350 while besieging Gibraltar, but he is hailed by the chronicler of these events as being the conqueror of numerous Muslim castles and towns, among them Priego.

It was in August 1341 that Alfonso, having already taken the nearby stronghold of Alcalá de Benzaide, moved to besiege Priego. With the help of siege engines and by means of mining its walls and towers, the attackers were able to overcome the town's defences within a matter of one or two weeks. This time, it was to remain definitively in Christian hands. The fortifications were quickly repaired, the town was provided with ample provisions and the Muslim population was expelled and in due course replaced by Christian settlers. In contrast with the situation which had existed after the town's capture by Fernando III, there was now a sense of permanence about its occupation and defence. Alfonso XI distributed land among seventy-four knights who had participated in the campaign. Among them will have figured, for example, Diego Ordóñez Zamorano, originating from the northern city of Zamora, who remained in the area as a settler and clearly showed considerable interest in the process of repopulating the town.[28] Not all was harmonious, however, and within four years territorial disputes had begun with neighbouring Alcalá.

Little is known of Priego's history in the following years, although we do hear a revealing tale of how in 1362 the governor of Zagra escaped when the town was being attacked by a Muslim army:

> Also, in the settlement at Zagra which he had just captured, the king left a squire called Fernán Delgadillo with a garrison of footsoldiers and crossbowmen. A few days later the Moors arrived and attacked Zagra, breaching the walls to such an extent that the castellan was forced to negotiate terms. On seeing that

---

[28] Carmona Ávila, 2004, 141; Peláez del Rosal and Quintanilla Raso, 121–22.

the Moors were breaking into the town, he arranged to be given safe conduct to Priego, which was in Christian hands, and made his way to the king in Alcaudete. King Pedro promptly had him executed.[29]

The king who ordered the execution of the unfortunate Fernán Delgadillo was Alfonso XI's only legitimate son, Pedro, famed for his brutality and known as 'Pedro the Cruel'.

King Pedro spent much of his reign caught up in a bitter conflict with his half-brothers and in particular the man who was finally to kill him and succeed to the throne as Enrique II. In the course of a civil war in which almost all of the kingdom became embroiled, Priego gave its support to Pedro in return for the granting of privileges and benefits, and following the king's death a number of the town's citizens took refuge with others of his supporters in the heavily fortified stronghold of Carmona. Enrique, although he eventually emerged victorious from the conflict, incurred huge debts towards both the noblemen of his own kingdom and the foreign mercenaries on whose assistance he had been heavily reliant. In many cases, their payment took the form of grants of property. Enrique had already granted lordship of Priego to Gonzalo Fernández de Córdoba at the time when he had first invaded Pedro's kingdom in 1366, and in 1370, the year after Pedro's death, this grant was confirmed: Priego ceased to be a royal possession and its lordship was granted to Gonzalo, a member of a distinguished family which had been established in the area of the Subbética since the time of its conquest by Fernando III. This branch of the Fernández de Córdoba family came to be known as the 'Casa (or Household) de Aguilar', named after the lordship of the town of Aguilar de la Frontera which it acquired under Gonzalo. The significance of these events for Priego's subsequent history was to be immense.

In due course, this family was also to assume the title of 'Casa de Priego', in spite of the fact that it was not resident in the town.

---

[29] Such, Vol II, 312–13.

Gonzalo Fernández de Córdoba now had the responsibility for defending Priego, still a frontier town, against incursions by the Moors of the kingdom of Granada, and along with the town and its castle, he also received all the possessions of the noblemen who had supported Pedro and had taken refuge in Carmona. In addition, he was paid a substantial sum for his services as well as receiving half of a payment (together with provisions) made by the monarchy to the town's citizens. In 1377, a *mayorazgo* was established by which the possessions of the lordship could under no circumstances be removed from the family.[30]

There could be no doubt with regard to the strategic importance that was attached to the protection of Priego and the surrounding area. Further evidence of this is the construction at some point after 1370 of the castle of Barcas, which stood at the confluence of the rivers Salado and Zagrilla. This fortification formed part of Priego's defensive network, controlling the route from Priego to Alcaudete and serving as a focal point for support of the *atalayas* or watchtowers situated at key points throughout the surrounding area.

When Gonzalo Fernández de Córdoba died in 1384, the lordship passed to his second son, Alfonso Fernández de Córdoba, whose principal concern over the next forty years was to be the defence of the frontier with the Muslim kingdom of Granada. After several years of peace, hostilities broke out at the beginning of the fifteenth century with a raid by Muḥammad VIII of Granada on Murcia. Following a heavy defeat suffered by the Christians at Los Collejares, east of Jaén, Priego found itself in danger of attack, and in both 1406 and 1407 the town sought assistance against the besieging Islamic forces. Alfonso Fernández de Córdoba took the lead in its defence, and it is possible that the Grand Master of the Order of Santiago also played a part in this campaign. Legend was to associate the town's relief on this occasion with the intervention of San

---

[30] A *mayorazgo* is an entailment which ensures that the whole of an inheritance goes to the firstborn heir.

Nicasio. This was the French Saint Nicaise or Nicasius, a bishop of Reims who was martyred by decapitation at the beginning of the fifth century AD and who, following his legendary role in saving Priego, was adopted as – and remains – the town's patron saint.

In 1421, in an elaborate ceremony, Alfonso's second son, Pedro Fernández de Córdoba, formally took possession of the castle and town of Priego, but he was to die in a skirmish on the frontier with Granada just three years later. Alfonso again assumed authority over the lordship, which on his death he passed on to his grandson, Pedro's son, also named Alfonso. However, by not respecting the rights of the line of his firstborn son (fundamental to the principle of *mayorazgo*), he was to set in motion a lengthy dispute. As a result, in 1427, King Juan II passed the responsibility for the defence of Priego, along with the substantial income that went with it, to his powerful and controversial favourite, Álvaro de Luna, Constable of Castile and Grand Master of the Order of Santiago. A lieutenant was appointed to carry out the duties and the post appears to have been returned to Alfonso by 1441, by which time the dispute over succession had been settled.

During this period, Priego witnessed another new and in the long term extremely significant development: the establishment in July 1426 of a brotherhood or *cofradía*, whose role was partly military and partly religious. At its head was Alfonso Fernández de Córdoba, and its members or *cofrades* also included both members of the clergy (among them the abbot of Alcalá la Real) and secular officials. The brotherhood took the name of San Ildefonso, a seventh-century archbishop of Toledo, and its purpose was to reinforce the town's capacity for defence against Muslim attack. The role of the clergy was simply to perform the appropriate rites annually on the day of San Ildefonso, attended by all the members of the brotherhood. The secular *cofrades* undertook to maintain horses ready for combat and were bound to avenge the death or capture of any other *cofrade* or member of his family by entering Muslim territory in order to take prisoners. This was a necessary response to a real danger. A number of other such brotherhoods were to be established in Priego later in the fifteenth century, but we have no information about how they were organised. None of them was to be long-lived, but others were to take their place. The *cofradías* of Priego were to go on to play a fundamental role in the town's history, long after the threat of Muslim aggression had ceased to exist.

Pedro Fernández de Córdoba, brother of Alfonso, was the next member of his family to take on the responsibility for Priego's defence. He was succeeded when he died in 1455 by his eight-year-old son, yet another Alfonso, who was to be best known by the title that he adopted, Don Alfonso de Aguilar. The town continued to be a bulwark of Christian Spain against Muslim Granada. At this stage, the war was largely being waged by local magnates rather than the monarchy, but we have details of the substantial payments still being made for the maintenance of the troops present in the town and also those in the castle of Barcas. The 1460s saw a civil war between the partisans of King Enrique IV and his brother Don Alfonso, and Don Alfonso de Aguilar's support for the latter was in due course rewarded by an increase in the payments allocated for the protection and upkeep of Priego, together with the castle of Barcas. As the final push to capture Granada gathered pace in the 1480s, Priego was essentially a gateway to the south and its direct involvement in the campaigns increased. At the same time, some inhabitants of Moorish towns such as Montefrío sought and received permission from Don Alfonso de Aguilar to settle in Priego. When Loja was captured in 1486, Boabdil, king of Granada but by this stage a puppet king in the hands of the Christians, was transferred for some time to Priego to be cured of his wounds. In the same year, Fernando and Isabel, the so-called Catholic Monarchs of Castile and Aragón, passed through the town on their way back to Córdoba following a series of military successes.

Don Alfonso de Aguilar died in 1501 while campaigning in

the Alpujarra mountains south of Granada. He had been a loyal servant of the Crown, and his family had made an important contribution to the lengthy and ultimately successful struggle to eliminate the remains of Muslim power from the Peninsula. It was his son and successor, Pedro Fernández de Córdoba, who was to reap the reward for this dedication, in the form of the creation by the Catholic Monarchs of the Marquisate of Priego. It is striking that among the various territories held by his family (the seat of which was in fact in Montilla), it was Priego, which had for so long occupied a strategically important position on a dangerous frontier, that was to give its name to the newly awarded honour. At the beginning of a new and radically different age, this was recognition of the vital role that the town had played over the preceding three centuries.

*

We have already seen how, following the recapture of Priego by Alfonso XI in 1341, the town and its territories were distributed among a group of knights who had accompanied the king on his campaign, and we know that four years later Alfonso dispatched his chamberlain, Diego Fernández, to Priego to find out how far the process of resettlement had progressed. Within months of its conquest, Priego received its royal charter, distinct from the original *fuero* awarded in the thirteenth century. This was accompanied by the granting to its citizens of a range of payments and the provision of a supply of wheat and barley, and also exemptions from tributes and taxes, including the *alcabala* or sales tax. New waves of settlers were attracted by these grants of privilege. Although from 1370 the people of Priego, as vassals of the House of Aguilar, found themselves liable to new taxes and other demands, the population continued to grow. In the years immediately following its recapture, Priego is reckoned to have had a population of about 900, but by the fifteenth century this had reached 1,500. Various disputes with neighbouring towns were finally settled, and ultimately the territory that came under Priego's jurisdiction was largely similar in extent to that which it takes in today. This territory stretched from a point north of the village of Zamoranos to just beyond Las Lagunillas in the south. To the east, however, it extended some way beyond both Fuente Tójar and Almedinilla to include the villages of La Rábita and Sileras and the rocky heights of Majalcorón.

The Priego community was made up of a mixture of professional soldiers and adventurers, agricultural workers and craftsmen who had to be prepared to take up arms when necessary. In the outlying areas, initially at least, the population probably continued to be predominantly Muslim. As we have already seen, the warlike conditions will have made agriculture difficult, except, for example, the keeping of livestock in the safer, more isolated areas of the hills. The fourteenth-century *Libro de la Montería*, a treatise on hunting attributed to King Alfonso XI, gives us a clear picture of the nature of the area: much of the land was still covered by Mediterranean forest, an ideal habitat for bears and wild boar. It seems that the only extensively cultivated land was situated close to the town in an area known as El Ruedo. The will of Gonzalo Fernández de Córdoba mentions the cultivation of vines, and we also know that the area immediately around the town produced cereals, fruit and vegetables as well as providing pasture for livestock. This land was, of course, extremely vulnerable to devastation by aggressors.

It is not known to what extent the Muslim population expelled after the town's conquest subsequently returned, although it is likely that some of it did. It is only in the late fifteenth century, in 1485, that we know for certain that some thirty families of 'Moors' were allowed to move under the protection of Don Alfonso de Aguilar from the Muslim territory of Montefrío to Priego. There, converted to Christianity, they were settled in a district close to the town walls, on land which was mostly marshy, and they devoted themselves principally to agriculture. By 1501, the number of these families had more than doubled, with the total number of converted Muslims resident in the town now reaching 300. In the course of the sixteenth century, such *Moriscos* would go on to make up a much larger and highly significant proportion of the population.[31]

*

In the course of the fourteenth century, the fortifications of the town were reinforced, in keeping with its essentially military character. The *Chronicle of Alfonso XI* tells us that by 1341 its ring of walls included several towers which were rebuilt after the siege. We also know that in the last third of the fourteenth century Gonzalo Fernández de Córdoba had ten towers built (or at least repaired) at his own expense in order to strengthen the defences. In the north east, there was the natural rampart known as the Adarve, reinforced by man-made towers. The river to the south, with its origin at the point now marked by the Fuente del Rey, added further protection. There were three gateways to the exterior, all defended by towers: in the south east, the Puerta del Sol; in the south west, the Arco (or Puerta) de Santa Ana; and in the north west, near to the castle, the Arco de San Bernardo. There were also a number of small gateways such as the now disappeared Arco de la Encarnación. The castle consisted of a walled perimeter, flanked by square towers and with its main tower – built in the second half of the thirteenth century – rising to a height of 30 metres and divided into three floors. It dates principally from the period when Priego belonged to the Order of Calatrava. It is probable that some further additions were made during the period in the fourteenth century when the town was again in Muslim hands, but on the whole the Muslim castle or *alcazaba* has been destroyed, pillaged and cannibalised beyond recognition.[32] Within and outside the

---

[31] The term *Morisco* is applied to members of the Muslim community who had converted to Christianity in the decades which followed the capture of Granada by the Christian forces in 1492.

[32] Carmona Ávila, Lunes Osuna and Moreno Rosa, 158.

walls of the castle there were several water deposits, one of which is clearly visible today.

In terms of ecclesiastical organisation, Priego came under the jurisdiction of the abbey of Alcalá la Real, which had been established immediately after the conquest of the town in 1341. Of the Christian churches of medieval Priego, the oldest – according to tradition – is that of Santiago, now disappeared but which was situated just to the east of the castle. This church appears to have already existed in the Muslim town.[33] Its existence is not, however, firmly documented until 1426, when the founders of the *cofradía* of San Ildefonso swore to honour it. Two other small churches also stood inside the walls: that of San Pedro, possibly built under the patronage of the Fernández de Córdoba family during the first half of the fifteenth century, and that of San Nicasio, built on the site of a mosque at the south-eastern limit of the walled area, where the church of La Aurora now stands. In neither case has the medieval building survived.[34] It has been suggested that the church of San Nicasio was founded to give thanks for the saint's protection of the town from plague. Near to the church there stood a hospice which attended to sick pilgrims and other travellers.[35] There is no evidence of the establishment of any monastic communities in Priego before the end of the fifteenth century, although there was a Franciscan hermitage towards Carcabuey which may well have dated back to the thirteenth century. However, it was in the following century that Priego's intense identification with the Christian faith was to leave an impressive and lasting mark on both the life and appearance of the town.

---

[33] Peláez del Rosal and Quintanilla Raso, 168.

[34] The church of San Pedro is said to have its origins in the 1220s, following the original conquest of Priego by Fernando III, but there is no firm evidence to support this.

[35] Peláez del Rosal and Quintanilla Raso, 168–69.

CHAPTER 4

The Forging of Priego

∞

On 2nd January 1492, King Boabdil, the last of the Nasrid sultans of Granada, formally surrendered his city and his kingdom to the Christian forces under the command of Isabel of Castile and Fernando of Aragón, known as Spain's Catholic Monarchs. In fact, the treaty of capitulation had been signed five weeks earlier. It was the culmination of a ten-year-long war of attrition, but for long before this there had been cross-border conflict which continued to pose a threat to frontier towns like Priego. For Christian Spain, the elimination of the danger represented by the last Muslim stronghold on the Peninsula gave cause for great celebration, and the accompanying emphasis on religious unity was fundamental to the sense of national identity and shared purpose, which the country's rulers sought to promote.

On the other hand, the continuing presence of a large Muslim population posed significant practical questions which were not to be resolved until the beginning of the seventeenth century. By the year 1500, the Muslims remaining in the Peninsula probably numbered half a million out of a total population of some seven to eight million, about half of them living in the old kingdom or emirate of Granada.[36] The terms on which Granada had been surrendered made generous promises to its Muslim inhabitants: they were to be allowed to continue to enjoy their possessions and their income in perpetuity and to retain both their religion and their customs, and their mosques would be respected. The promises were, however, soon broken, and hard-line policies provoked a rebellion of the Muslims of Granada in 1499. These events had an immediate and direct effect on Priego, which still

---

[36] Matthew Carr, 53.

found itself close to the front line of conflict. A reminder of this is the pennant awarded to the *prieguense* nobleman Juan Martín de Zamorano for saving the life of Pedro Fernández de Córdoba, heir to the lordship of Aguilar, during a disastrous campaign carried out in 1501 in territory which had previously belonged to the kingdom of Granada. The figure of Santiago (Saint James), known as Matamoros (the Moor-Slayer), dominates the pennant, clear evidence indeed that peace and tolerance remained a distant dream.[37] Within a decade of the city's capture by Fernando and Isabel, the Moors of the kingdom of Castile, of which Granada now formed part, were being forced to convert to Christianity. These new Christians, now known as *Moriscos*, would increasingly become subject to both suspicion and harassment and, in due course, these events were to have a marked and long-lasting effect on the development of Priego.

The pennant of the Zamorano family
This pennant was awarded to the *prieguense* nobleman Juan Martín de Zamorano in recognition of his heroic action in saving the life of Pedro Fernández de Córdoba, heir to the lordship of Aguilar, while campaigning against the Moors of Granada in 1501. The pennant depicts Pedro Fernández (on the ground) and the coat of arms of his father, Don Alfonso, but it is dominated by the figure of Santiago (Saint James), in his characteristic role as *Matamoros* (the Moor-Slayer). It reflects the hostile nature of relationships between Christians and Muslims a decade after the surrender of Granada in 1492. *The author is grateful to Rafael Carmona for his permission to use this photograph.*

---

[37] For a detailed analysis of these events and the significance of the pennant, see Carmona Ávila, 2004.

The reign of the Catholic Monarchs saw radical changes in the nature of Spanish society. For Priego, the beginning of the new century was likewise marked by a development which was to have considerable long-term consequences. In 1501, the Catholic Monarchs, in recognition of the loyal service that his ancestors had done to the town, elevated Pedro Fernández de Córdoba III (the man whose life had been saved by Juan Martín de Zamorano) to the rank of marquis, and he took the title of Marquis of Priego. This was considered one of the most distinguished noble titles in Spain, and the prestige of his lineage was to be further enhanced at the beginning of the eighteenth century by its union with the illustrious house of Medinaceli. It is not known for certain why Pedro Fernández chose Priego for his title out of the eleven towns that made up his lordship (he was a member of the House of Aguilar and the family had been more closely associated with the town of Montilla), but, as has already been pointed out, it is probably because, having been the one most closely situated to the frontier with the kingdom of Granada, it was the most representative of the family's military role.

The treatment of the citizens of Priego by the marquis and his successors cannot, however, be defined as entirely benevolent. Over the following centuries, until the abolition of seignorial rights – essentially that of the feudal system – in 1837, their treatment of the town community was in some respects characterised by exploitation and abuse. Nor was the relationship of the first marquis with the monarchy entirely straightforward: in 1508, in the course of the resolution of a long-standing dispute over the ownership and use of land, Don Pedro Fernández arrested an investigating judge and had him imprisoned in Montilla. King Fernando in his fury had the castle decommissioned and ordered Don Pedro to be exiled from Córdoba and a castle governor – Gonzalo Ruiz de Figueroa – to be appointed.[38] Within two years, however, all of the marquis's possessions and honours had been restored,

---

[38] Peláez del Rosal and Rivas Carmona, 85–89.

and it was in the years following this episode that Don Pedro founded the Franciscan convent of San Esteban. It was later to become generally known as the convent of San Francisco. When he died in 1517, he left his elder daughter, Doña Catalina Fernández de Córdoba, his title and the income from his extensive estates. Doña Catalina was to be distinguished as a patron of the arts, and for Priego the period until her death in 1569 was to be marked by growth and conspicuous urban development.

The cloister of the convent of San Francisco (originally known as San Esteban)

The convent was founded in 1510. Its construction, together with that of its church, was largely completed by 1548, although work on them continued into the eighteenth century. After its disentailment in 1835, the convent building was put to a variety of social and industrial uses, and by 1902 it was being used as a workshop by a textile company. In the later twentieth century, it fell into total disrepair, but it was subsequently restored and transformed into a hotel. *Photograph by Antonio Jesús Villena.*

Don Pedro died just one year after the succession to the Spanish throne of the first of the country's Habsburg rulers, Carlos I (who also became Holy Roman Emperor as Charles V).[39] Spain was embarking upon a new stage in its development and so was Priego. Nationally, this was a time of rapid economic growth, built on an extended period of peace in the Peninsula, greater integration into European trade and the benefits brought by the conquest and colonisation of Spain's territories in the Americas. Agricultural production increased rapidly to keep pace with a growing population. There was notable development of industry, for example, that based on the production of silk, particularly important in the old kingdom of Granada, which retained a large population of Muslim origin. Initially, the greatest beneficiaries of this prosperity were Spain's nobility, who enjoyed much of the income from both the land and the commerce in the towns. The Church remained both powerful and wealthy, but the need for moral and educational reform was widely recognised. The Council of Trent, held in Italy in 1545, would provide the stimulus for reform and innovation, and the effects of this on Priego's society and institutions would be felt for centuries to come.

In the early decades of the sixteenth century, Priego had about 4,500 inhabitants, but by the time of the 1587 census the figure had reached 8,000.[40] The increase was further boosted by the arrival of a large number of *Moriscos*, but also by immigrants from Portugal.[41] Over the same period, the surface area of the town more or less doubled. Initially, it was still largely contained within its medieval

---

[39] The House of Habsburg (or House of Austria) was one of the principal dynasties of Europe. It was founded in the eleventh century, and from 1440 to the mid-eighteenth century its members continuously occupied the throne of the Holy Roman Empire. Carlos inherited the Spanish throne through the marriage of his mother, Juana I of Castile, to his father, the Habsburg Archduke Philip 'the Handsome'.

[40] Cobo Calmaestra, 8. Such figures are approximate, as census figures are based on the number of *vecinos* or heads of family. The principle usually followed is to assume an average of four people in each family.

[41] Vera Aranda, 137.

walls, but as the population grew (partly the result of the exemption from taxes on agricultural produce enjoyed by its citizens), a new suburb quickly developed towards the south and west. The removal of the threat of attack from Granada provided the secure conditions necessary for agriculture and much more land around the town was now cultivated, with the production of cereals and olive oil increasing considerably.

Nevertheless, the town's citizens did not find it at all easy to participate directly in the running of municipal affairs and to free themselves from the firm grip that the marquisate had established on commerce and on the provision of services. The governor appointed by the marquis had almost total control over the administrative and judicial systems of the town.[42] Moreover, a substantial proportion of the land in the municipal area belonged to the marquisate, and many of the citizens were effectively its tenants or otherwise in its debt. In 1526, a judge sent by the Diocese of Jaén visited Priego to report on the nature of the financial rights claimed by the marquis, and his findings are revealing.[43] Within the town, the representatives of the lordship owned various inns and taverns, all the shops in the square, the mills and the bakeries, the tannery and the fulling mill. They controlled prices and levied a tax of 10% on items sold. Effectively, the marquisate had a monopoly of all services and trade within the town. The judge ruled that the rights and freedoms of the town's citizens should be respected, but the situation remained more or less unchanged. In spite of a number of petitions and appeals, the disputes over such exploitation and abuses were to drag on throughout the century and beyond.

In 1525, a reorganisation of the town's council (the *cabildo*) led to the production, from that point on, of a regular record of its meetings, thus giving us for the first time a real insight into the community's life.[44] Over the centuries, these municipal minutes

---

[42] Durán Alcalá, 156

[43] Peláez del Rosal and Rivas Carmona, 96.

[44] Ibid 92–94.

have been the principal source of much of our information about developments in the town. From them, for example, we learn of the death and burial four years later of the *marquesa*'s husband, who fell victim of the plague which devastated the community and caused the town's gates to be shut. On a much more positive note, during this period, we read of a series of important practical decisions: the setting-up of a granary and a grain market in order to ensure the supply of bread to the people of the town; the extension of the municipal slaughterhouse; the creation of a prison and a courtroom; and the enlargement of the square outside the castle walls. There are also reports of the dispatch of fifteen knights from the town to serve with the king's army in France, and the expulsion of vagrants (including *Moriscos*) who had been moving into the town in large numbers. These developments are all evidence of a sense of initiative and direction and of the creation of a municipal identity, reflecting the increase in the size of the town's population and its growing prosperity.

The increasing wealth of the town was reflected by the construction of new thoroughfares which transformed its appearance, existing alongside a warren of narrow and irregular streets. This became particularly striking as the town extended beyond the old walled area, with the creation of arteries such as those corresponding to Calle Río (or la Calle del Río), Calle Carrera de la Monjas, Calle Ribera and Calle Málaga.[45] To the west, the urban area stretched out towards what became known as the height of El Calvario.

The sixteenth century saw the construction of a number of important buildings, both secular and religious. Prominent among these was the new municipal grain store, the Pósito (also known as La Alhóndiga), an impressive building constructed in the Mannerist style between 1572 and 1576.[46] It replaced the

---

[45] Vera Aranda, 137–38.

[46] Mannerism in architecture was a style of Italianate origin which emphasised elegance, ingenuity and self-conscious artifice.

grain store built some thirty years earlier and it survived until the 1930s. It was situated in what is now the square of El Palenque, which between 1566 and 1574 was transformed from a spot described as 'dirty and unhealthy' into a central point in the town on which several streets converged.[47] The development of this area illustrates the extent to which the town was now extending towards the west. El Palenque was used to stage a variety of public events, including theatre, executions, acts organised by the Holy Inquisition and also (from 1566) bullfights.[48]

The attractive building known as the Carnicerías Reales was completed just three years after the Pósito to house the municipal slaughterhouse and meat market and still stands today in the area known as the Huerta Palacio, just below the castle, where it was built to take advantage of an underground stream originating at the Fuente del Rey. Like the Pósito, the Carnicerías Reales was constructed in the Italianate Mannerist style and embodied the aspirations to elegance and distinction which now characterised the burgeoning town of Priego. In the same period, new municipal buildings were constructed in the square then known as the Plaza de los Escribanos (now Llano de la Iglesia) in the heart of the old town, thus establishing a prestigious home for the representatives of the citizens alongside those of the nobility (the castle) and the Church. A new corn exchange and a prison were also built in the area, which was now firmly established as the town's administrative centre.

The first step in the creation of what was to become an iconic feature of the town was completed in 1586. The fountain

---

[47] Alférez Molina, 139.

[48] Carmona Ávila, 2005, 115, and Vera Aranda, 139–40. For an account of the bullfights held in El Palenque, see Forcada Serrano, 1992, 14–17. In fact, the first written record of a bullfight in Priego relates to 1528, as part of the celebration of the recovery from illness of the husband of the *marquesa*. This event took place outside what was then the chapel of San Nicasio (now the church of La Aurora). See Forcada Serrano, 1992, 14.

which originally bore the name of the Fuente del Rey ('King's Fountain') became known as the Fuente de la Salud ('Fountain of Health') because its waters were believed to have curative properties during periods of plague.[49] It was almost certainly designed by the Italian-trained Mannerist architect Francisco del Castillo, who is likely also to have worked on the Pósito and the Carnicerías Reales, and the distinguished local stonemason Alonso González Bailén also played a prominent part in its construction. The fountain marked the source of the river, and until this point the area around it had been a 'pestilent mud-pit'.[50] The town council also purchased agricultural land along the course of the river as it flowed down from the Fuente (corresponding more or less to the direction of the modern Calle Río), and the final decade of the century saw the river's canalisation. The way was prepared for the orderly construction of new dwellings along its banks, and the process of canalisation was an important step towards the effective exploitation of the abundance of water. The benefits were to include the provision of a reliable supply of water for the needs of the town's population and also, by means of numerous underground networks, for services such as the milling of flour, the dying of cloth and the irrigation of sugar cane and mulberry trees.[51] Priego had become increasingly prosperous and also ambitious, and the modern town was beginning to take shape.

---

[49] The king after whom the fountain was originally named was Alfonso XI who, according to legend, before launching his assault on the town, pitched his camp outside the walls in the area of the spring.

[50] Vera Aranda, 140.

[51] Alférez Molina, 2004, 145.

Las Carnicerías Reales ('the Royal Meat Market') was constructed between 1576 and 1579. It was designed by Francisco del Castillo ('the younger'), a Spanish architect (born in Jaén) who had studied in Italy. A stone spiral staircase leads down to the basement, where the animals were slaughtered. *Photograph by Antonio Jesús Villena.*

The sixteenth century also saw far-reaching events affecting the religious life of the town's community. As we have already seen, in 1510, the marquis of Priego, Pedro Fernández de Córdoba, established the convent of San Esteban, which was largely completed over the following four decades, at the same time as the surrounding area was being transformed. The convent of San Esteban was soon to house the town's first community of Observant Franciscans, destined to play a vital and dynamic role in developing the spiritual life of Priego's citizens and in determining the character of the town over the centuries.[52] As members of a mendicant order, potentially representing a burden on the resources of the community, the Franciscans were

---

[52] Observant Franciscans, also known as the Order of Friars Minor or simply Franciscans, are a mendicant religious Order which was originally established in 1209 by Saint Francis of Assisi.

at first met with a degree of suspicion, but they were soon to be thoroughly integrated into its life.[53] The convent acquired much of the agricultural land surrounding it, as well as receiving a substantial part of the alms given by the people of the town. The church of San Francisco, adjacent to the convent, was completed in about 1548. At this stage, it was a renaissance-gothic construction, but it was to be remodelled in a more flamboyant Baroque style in the seventeenth and eighteenth centuries. The square outside the church, known as El Compás, came to be used for a wide range of religious functions of central importance in the life of the town.

Also of fundamental significance for Priego's spiritual life was the construction of what was to be the town's principal place of worship. Writing at the end of the eighteenth century, Pedro Alcalá-Zamora explains the background:

> Following the conquest of the town of Priego, a church was established under the advocacy of Santiago, situated to the east of the castle and facing its curtain wall. It was a church consisting of three low and narrow naves, but once the community spread beyond the walled area it became necessary to build a church with a greater capacity in a setting which offered more space, in order to achieve the full extent of its destiny.[54]

The church of Santiago had not occupied the same site as its replacement but a smaller one adjacent to the castle. The new church, begun in 1525 and largely completed by about 1550, was to be the parish church of Nuestra Señora de la Asunción. It was built in a late gothic style with elements of *mudéjar* decoration.[55] In the eighteenth century, this late gothic church would be

---

[53] Forcada Serrano, 2000, 25.

[54] Alcalá-Zamora, 11. The printed text in fact has no page numbers and these have been added by hand.

[55] The term *mudéjar* is applied to architectural and decorative features associated with the art of Muslim Spain, but it does not necessarily imply the involvement of craftsmen of Muslim origin.

remodelled into the spectacular Baroque construction which can be seen today, just as the *ermita* of San Antonio Abad, also probably begun in the 1540s, was to be rebuilt as the Iglesia de las Mercedes which now stands in the Calle Carrera de las Monjas.[56]

Outside the town, it seems that the second half of the sixteenth century saw the establishment of the *ermita* of Santo Cristo del Humilladero (known to have been in existence by 1593). Built on a hill overlooking the town from the south-west, it offered a place for the pious traveller to pray before entering or leaving Priego. This was to be the site of the *ermita* known as El Calvario, dating from the beginning of the eighteenth century but rebuilt in 1939. As the destination of the Good Friday procession, it continues today to play an important part in the devotional life of the town community.

From the middle of the sixteenth century there was a growing emphasis on the promotion of religious festivals, notably that of Corpus Christi which, with its vivid and colourful dances, music and dramatic events, was celebrated with particular brilliance in Priego and was characterised by conspicuous displays of popular devotion. The importance given to it may well reflect the influence of the preacher and theologian San Juan de Ávila, who is known to have spent some time in Priego together with other distinguished clerics and scholars such as Fray Luis de Granada.[57] The saint's influence also undoubtedly contributed to the foundation of the Colegio de San Nicasio, established in the 1560s and situated next to what is now the church of La Aurora. This school was intended to teach the rudiments of reading and writing to young children and specifically those of converted

---

[56] An *ermita* was originally a hermitage, a place of retreat and prayer, usually associated with an individual friar or hermit or a very small community. However, the term came to be applied more generally to a chapel, small church or sanctuary situated in an isolated spot. An *ermita* would not be used for worship on a regular basis, but it was customary for a mass to be said there on the day of the saint to whom it was dedicated.

[57] Peláez del Rosal and Rivas Carmona, 94–95.

Muslims living in the Barrio de la Villa.[58] There is evidence here that the influx of new Christians gave an added impulse to the cultural life of the town and also that there was a close connection between the old Muslim quarter and the area occupied by the convent.[59] As was pointed out in the previous chapter, the church of La Aurora itself probably dates back to the end of the fifteenth century and was initially dedicated to San Nicasio. It had been built on a site previously occupied by a mosque.

It has already been seen how the *cofradía* (or brotherhood) of San Ildefonso had been founded in the early fifteenth century to contribute to the defence of Priego against attacks from the Muslim kingdom of Granada and how it had combined military and spiritual functions. We also know that in 1495 there existed in Priego a number of *cofradías* connected with trade guilds and that in 1509 a brotherhood by the name of La Santa Caridad ('Holy Charity') provided lodging for the poor, for pilgrims and for the sick.[60] There is evidence that from the moment of their establishment in Priego the Franciscans attempted to promote the creation of *cofradías*.[61] The first of these seems to have been that of the Limpia Concepción de la Virgen María ('The Pure Conception of the Virgin Mary'), which was in existence by about 1520 but was short-lived. It was, however, towards the middle of the sixteenth century that the religious impulse which was to lead to the Council of Trent (1545–63) brought about a marked change of emphasis in the character and functions of such bodies.[62] The first of the *cofradías de penitencia* ('brotherhoods of penance') to be founded in Priego during this period was that of La Santa Vera Cruz ('The Holy True Cross'), which dates from 1550.

---

[58] For an account of the school's role, see Peláez del Rosal, 2000.
[59] Alférez Molina, 2004, 147.
[60] Peláez de Rosal and Quintanilla Raso, 70–71; Alférez Molina, 73.
[61] Forcada Serrano, 2000, 28.
[62] For the Council of Trent, see page 52, above.

Devotion to the Cross and the episode of Christ's scourging had already been widespread during the Middle Ages, but it was in the mid-sixteenth century that brotherhoods devoted to the True Cross began to proliferate in Spain and particularly in Andalucía. On 1st April 1550, the abbot of Alcalá la Real gave his authorisation for the establishment of the *cofradía* in Priego and, in spite of an early dispute with the convent over lost revenue, the body's initial constitution was rapidly approved. The terms of this document dealt principally with procedures and the responsibilities of the *cofrades*: admission to the brotherhood; the obligation to attend Mass and confession on Maundy Thursday; fasting; taking part in a procession and performing the necessary acts of discipline, including flagellation; attendance at other masses and celebrations, including those of the Holy Cross in May and the Exaltation in September; attendance at the burial of the brothers; visiting the sick and dying; payments and penalties; brothers who leave Priego; the appointment of officials; a prohibition on bearing arms; observing secrecy; seeking alms; and obedience.[63]

The Cofradía de la Vera Cruz was quick to flourish and gain in prestige, and evidence of this is the bull granted in Rome by Cardinal Alejandro Farnesio in 1576, conceding numerous graces and indulgences to its members. The Maundy Thursday processions through the streets, a dramatic and bloody affair, became one of the most powerful events in the life of the town. Then, towards the end of the century, a new tradition was born. On 19th May 1593, in response to a prolonged period of drought, the members of the *cofradía* took part in a procession to plead for rain. This was probably the origin of the May processions which still take place. It was also significant because a week later it was imitated by the members of another, newly founded, brotherhood, Esclavos del Santísimo Sacramento y Naçareos de Priego ('Slaves of the Holiest Sacrament and Nazarenes of Priego'), also known as La Hermandad de Jesús Nazareno.[64]

---

[63] Forcada Serrano, 2000, 37–41.

[64] Ibid., 52. The terms *cofradía* and *hermandad* are essentially synonymous and are here applied to organisations which are religious in character but are made up of lay members.

Like the Cofradía de la Santa Vera Cruz, this brotherhood was – and continues to be – centred on the church of San Francisco. A third *cofradía*, which was founded towards the end of the sixteenth century in Priego and in several other towns in the diocese of Córdoba, was that of the Santo Entierro de Cristo y María Santísima de la Soledad ('The Holy Burial of Christ and the Holiest Mary of Solitude'). It was linked originally to the old chapel of San Luis outside the town walls. Its members' duties included the collection of the sick and of dead bodies from the streets and assistance to the ill, to orphans and to the poor.

These *cofradías* were rapidly becoming established as part of Priego's social fabric, and others which were to be prominent in later centuries may well have had their roots in this earlier period.[65]

In the case of the Hermandad de Jesús Nazareno, it is argued that it was more truly representative of the social structure of the town than the Cofradía de la Vera Cruz as it recruited from any social class.[66] One social group, however, was specifically barred from membership: *Moriscos* and new Christians, who, by the end of the sixteenth century made up a surprisingly large part of Priego's population.

*

We have seen how by the beginning of the sixteenth century there was already a group of about thirty families of Muslim origin living in Priego, having been brought there under the protection of Don Alfonso de Aguilar following the capture of Montefrío by the Christian forces. They lived in an area in the

---

[65] There seems, for example, to have been a Cofradía del Rosario ('Brotherhood of the Rosary') in existence in 1580, associated with the church of Santiago. Several years later, its role was taken on by another body of the same name, based in what was initially the chapel of San Nicasio but later became the church of La Aurora. It is as La Virgen de la Aurora ('the Virgin of the Dawn') that the *cofradía* is known today. See Alférez Molina, 78.

[66] Ibid., 89.

extreme south west of the old town, which came to be known as La Morería. This was one of the most prominent communities of its kind in Andalucía, and it was to continue to be so until the beginning of the seventeenth century. By 1502, ten years after the fall of Granada, it had grown to include some seventy-seven families, amounting to a total of 301 people.[67] There is also a striking suggestion of quite extensive intermarriage in what we are told of the inhabitants of Priego at the time of the foundation of the Franciscan convent: that many of them were 'of bad character and dishonourable blood because they were descendants of Moors or had been converted to our faith'.[68]

In 1502, the Moors of the kingdom of Granada were forced to choose between conversion to Christianity and exile, and the large number of new Christians of Muslim origin were subjected to increasingly intense harassment which was to lead eventually to the outbreak of a bloody conflict. As these *Moriscos* continued to abandon Granada, Priego, with an already established Moorish community, proved a particularly attractive place of refuge. With them, the *Moriscos* brought valuable new skills, introducing the cultivation of the mulberry and the breeding of silk worms.

When the *Morisco* uprising took place in the Alpujarras in 1568, Priego saw itself under threat on account of its proximity to Granada. A militia was raised, consisting of one hundred citizens, and measures were taken to repair Priego's walls and gateways and the watchtowers in the surrounding area. Priego also contributed troops to Don Juan de Austria's campaigns in the Alpujarras.[69] By 1570, with the confrontation at an end, mass deportation of the *Morisco* population of the old kingdom of Granada began. The marquis of Priego saw this as an

---

[67] Cobo Calmaestra, 8.

[68] Peláez del Rosal, 1960, 9.

[69] Ibid., 11. Don Juan was an illegitimate son of Carlos I. He was a distinguished military commander best known for his victory over the Ottoman fleet in the battle of Lepanto.

opportunity to increase the town's workforce, and he actively sought to attract more *Moriscos*. This approach was at odds with the Crown's policy of dispersing the Moorish community and breaking down the heavy concentrations of *Moriscos* which were to be found in some parts of Andalucía. Essentially, the problem was that, although the converted Moors were nominally Christians, there was considerable suspicion with regard to the genuineness of that conversion. Those living in Priego (of whom there were some 500) were ordered to go to Córdoba but on the suspension of the decree they were able to return. The town council's solution to the problem of preventing the creation of an unintegrated population of *Moriscos* was to move them out from the Morería and into the Christian community. Relationships between those of Muslim origin and the established Christian population were generally harmonious, but there are records of cases of the Inquisition prosecuting *Moriscos* suspected of Islamic practices, for example, Isabel de Trujillo, who was accused of forbidding people to give her daughter bacon to eat or speaking to her of the name of Jesus.[70] Very few of Priego's *Moriscos* could aspire to acquire lands of their own, and most of them worked in agriculture, as artisans, as tradesmen or in some cases as muleteers.[71]

There can be no doubt that the rapid growth of the silk, or more precisely taffeta, industry in Priego was in part at least the result of the presence in the town of the skilled *Morisco* workers. This had the additional advantage that it enabled the townspeople to work independently of the control exercised by the marquis, although by the beginning of the seventeenth century the trade was subject to tighter regulation and to supervision by an official inspector. Certainly, the industry continued to flourish, and in the seventeenth and eighteenth

---

[70] Aranda Doncel, 339. For an account of the prosecutions by the Inquisition of inhabitants of Priego accused of Islamic or Jewish practices, see Alférez Molina, 2000, 52–56.

[71] Cobo Calmaestra, 13.

centuries it was to serve as the mainspring of Priego's economy.

The positive nature of the relationship between the old Christians and the *Moriscos* in Priego was in marked contrast with the political situation in Spain as a whole. While nationally pressure was mounting for a general expulsion from the country of all converted Muslims, in Priego, so relaxed was the situation that in 1586, on the occasion of a visit by the marquis to the town, the council decided that two companies of troops were to be drawn up, one of them consisting of *Moriscos* in traditional dress.[72] Nevertheless, in 1609, the Council of State finally took the decision that a general expulsion was to be enforced. In due course, the entire community being expelled from Priego set off for the port of Málaga. Concerned at the economic loss that this would imply, the lords and nobles of Priego, including the abbot of Alcalá la Real, pleaded for their exemption on the grounds of their impeccable religious conduct, and the *Moriscos* were ordered to return to Priego. The number involved is recorded as 1,768.[73] In 1611, Felipe III issued a new edict and in consequence some 300 *Moriscos*, residents of La Morería, were again obliged to leave. Later in the same year, all those remaining were expelled, and in total the town, against its will, had lost a quarter of its 12,000 inhabitants.

Along with the effects of the outbreaks of plague which occurred in the late sixteenth and early seventeenth centuries, this draconian act of intolerance left Priego's workforce seriously depleted. The *Morisco* community, the origins of which went back some 125 years, had left a firm and lasting mark on the town, and in particular it had implanted in it a textile industry which, in one form or another, was to remain at the centre of Priego's economy until the second half of the twentieth century.

---

[72] Ibid., 14.
[73] Aranda Doncel, 164.

CHAPTER 5

Baroque Splendour

~~

The final decade of the sixteenth century had seen a serious deterioration in Priego's level of prosperity. Trade had begun to decline as a result of international conflicts, and as the new century began, the position was worsened by the threat of plague and by the weight of taxes demanded by the Crown as a contribution to the improvement of coastal defences. There can be no doubt that the loss of a quarter of the town's population in the following years through the expulsión of the *Moriscos* dealt it a further massive blow.

These were times of serious financial difficulty. Moreover, in 1611, the council had to deal with a further heavy tax demand: Priego was now expected to pay (with limited exceptions for agricultural produce) the *alcabala* or sales tax from which it had previously been considered exempt as a result of rights granted by Alfonso XI when the town was recaptured from the Muslims in 1341. The conclusion of the legal battle which ensued was that the town was to purchase for the considerable sum of 130,000 *ducados* (the present equivalent of which is about 22 million euros) the right to enjoy this exemption, administering the tax itself, and also to work and sell silk in perpetuity. Payment was to be made in instalments. The agreement was approved by King Felipe III in 1617 and ratified in 1621, and it was subsequently confirmed by Felipe IV. The long-term consequence of this, however, was that, when the payments fell into arrears, the resulting costs proved a drain on the finances of the town and its people over the following two centuries.[74] The

---

[74] Peláez Rosal and Rivas Carmona, 120–24.

situation was further complicated by the rampant inflation which bedevilled the Spanish economy in the seventeenth century. The financial hardship caused to the town by the *alcabala* question was already in evidence when it was cited in the council's records for 1631 as one of the reasons for rejecting the establishment of an Augustinian convent, probably in the Calle Cava.[75] The council's records tell us that by 1763 just under half of the 130,000 *ducados* had been repaid and emphasise the serious harm being done by the debt to the wellbeing of the town and to its industry.

The financial problems of the seventeenth century were certainly not limited to Priego. Nationally, this was a period of decadence both politically and economically. The reign of Felipe IV (1621–65) was marked by the Thirty Years War, with conflict against France continuing until 1659. Spain's position in Europe was seriously weakened, and the economic supremacy of the Spanish Empire was increasingly challenged by the Dutch and the English. There were rebellions in Cataluña and in Portugal, and in 1641 Priego was required to contribute men of noble birth to the Spanish army to take part in these conflicts. The country's problems continued to multiply during the regency of Mariana of Austria and the reign of Carlos II, who was troubled throughout by serious illness. For much of the seventeenth century, the monarchy's finances were in a constant state of crisis and, although imports of bullion from the Americas continued to increase, most of this income was paid over to foreign creditors. Over a period which was also marked by repeated poor harvests and outbreaks of plague, Spain's population fell by almost a quarter between 1600 and 1680. In Andalucía, the period around 1680 was marked by a particular crisis: this was the year of a serious earthquake with its epicentre in Málaga which caused damage throughout the region (it brought down part of Priego's prison building), but these years were also marked by a combination of violent storms and long

---

[75] Ibid., 118.

periods of drought. The price of bread soared and hunger spread.[76] In Priego itself, plague struck in 1651 and in 1680. The second of these occasions followed a number of years of very poor harvests which had obliged the town to buy bread elsewhere at exorbitant prices.

However, it was against this apparently gloomy background that the spiritual life of Priego was to be transformed by the establishment of important new institutions. An early step was the foundation in 1617 at the instigation of the *marquesa* of Priego, Doña Juana Enríquez de Ribera, of a Franciscan Clarist convent.[77] The community of nuns, of which Doña Juana's sister was the founding abbess, was a substantial one, numbering fifty-four from the outset, and donations and legacies contributed considerably to its development. It was housed in the convent of Santa Clara (also known as San Antonio), which was constructed in the central square where the town hall now stands, near to what was then the Puerta del Agua. And later in the century, in 1659, a community of Discalced Franciscans (the branch of the Order known as *alcantarinos*) was established in what had been the *ermita* of San Luis. This was situated outside the town (on a site described as 'insalubrious'), where the church had been newly restored. In 1664, however, they moved to the more central site of the *ermita* of San Pedro.[78] Work began immediately on the construction of the church, which stands there today, and this was completed in 1690, although its interior continued to be elaborated over the course of the following century.

In 1637, moreover, another very significant act of foundation took place when a nobleman called Don Juan de Herrera left all his wealth to pay for the establishment of a hospice for the poor of the town community. This took the name of San Onofre. It was situated in the centre of the town, very close to the convent of

---

[76] Forcada Serrano, 2000, 82.

[77] The Clarists, also known as Poor Clares, were contemplative nuns, the second branch of the Franciscan Order to be established.

[78] For an explanation of the term *ermita*, see Chapter 4, note 56.

Santa Clara. When it was later taken over by the brothers of the Order of San Juan de Dios, it took from them the name – el Convento-Hospital de San Juan de Dios – by which (now a home for the elderly) it is still known. The church of the foundation was rebuilt at the beginning of the eighteenth century and was further elaborated over the following fifty years, to form part of Priego's rich Baroque heritage.[79] Together, the three convents formed a religious enclave that dominated the centre of Priego.

Another sign of the intense spiritual life of the town was the continuing development of the religious brotherhoods known as *cofradías* or *hermandades*. Their influence over the life of Priego has been immense, and they continue today to play a highly conspicuous role in the life of the community. It was during the period generally associated with cultural influences known as 'Baroque' that their activities acquired the dramatic colour and emotive force which were to take so firm a hold over the public imagination. A Priego historian describes the social and cultural background:

> In the seventeenth century, the religious Confraternities associated with Holy Week acquired their full force and splendour, becoming steeped in the Baroque just like all the arts which contributed to the character of this period. The regeneration of the religious Orders followed the directives of the Council of Trent: a religious society conceived in terms of a dualism embracing the catastrophic and the festive, a Church which had been renewed by the spirit of the Counter-Reformation, and the art which was created as a result. All of this combined to produce processions which were so

---

[79] The term 'Baroque' is used in the course of this chapter in a number of different contexts. When it is applied to the visual arts, including architecture and sculpture, it is usually associated with the use of exuberant and flamboyant detail to create a sense of awe. It implies a dramatic effect and the use of ornate, even sensuous, decoration, and in this respect it was consciously used by the Church to appeal to both the emotions and the senses of the faithful. In the visual arts, Baroque is generally associated with the period between the early seventeenth century and about 1740, although in Priego the style continued to flourish well after this.

spectacular as to make the people share in the experience of the days commemorating Christ's passion, in accordance with the ideology of a society seeking to impress and itself be impressed by its festive and religious practices.[80]

We have already seen how the Cofradía de la Santa Vera Cruz was established in the mid-sixteenth century and how what was to become the Hermandad del Nazareno ('Brotherhood of the Nazarene') was founded in 1593 under the title of 'Slaves of the Holiest Sacrament and Nazarenes of Priego' and refounded in 1669. Both brotherhoods were based initially in the Franciscan convent of San Esteban, while the Cofradía de Nuestra Señora de la Soledad ('Brotherhood of Our Lady of Solitude') had its chapel in the church of San Pedro Apóstol. The third of these organisations had been first established in 1594 and was refounded ninety years later. Its initial constitution included the requirement for its members to take part in a penitential procession on Good Friday, and it was such dramatic events that were at the centre of the brotherhoods' activities.

A number of other brotherhoods came into existence during the course of the seventeenth century. The Real Cofradía de María Santísima de los Desamparados y Santísimo Cristo de la Expiración ('Royal Confraternity of the Holiest Mary of the Helpless and the Holiest Christ in his Moment of Death') had its roots in the sixteenth century in connection with a hospice for the poor, but its formal constitution was not drawn up until 1632. The Hermandad de Jesús en su Entrada Triunfal a Jerusalén ('Brotherhood of Jesus on his Triumphant Entry into Jerusalem'), dedicated to the celebration of Palm Sunday, had fully developed its ceremonial by the second half of the seventeenth century, and the authorisation for its foundation was given in 1670. The establishment of the Hermandad de Nuestra Señora del Buen Suceso ('Brotherhood of Our Lady of Good Favour') was officially approved in 1690, although its

---

[80] Alférez Molina, 97.

origins appear to go back some thirty years before that date. The previous year had seen the approval of the constitution of the Cofradía de María Santísima de los Dolores ('Confraternity of the Holiest Mary of the Sorrows'), although its origins, linked to the veneration of an image of Mary at the foot of the Cross, go back to the Middle Ages; and also founded in 1689 was the Cofradía de las Benditas Ánimas del Purgatorio ('Confraternity of the Blessed Souls in Purgatory').

The core of the brotherhoods' activity was participation in public acts of worship: masses, sermons and, most conspicuously, processions, characterised by an atmosphere of popular devotion. Some provided care and assistance to the poor and the sick, often through alms and donations, but in general their principal social concern was centred on giving help to the dying and their families, help which was both practical and spiritual. This was directed in the first instance at fellow members but was also extended to the surrounding community.[81]

A number of the brotherhoods founded at this time did not survive beyond the more critical years of the eighteenth century, but some of them have continued to play a fundamental role in the lives and beliefs of the people of Priego up to the present day. In view of their great significance, it is worth looking in detail at the nature of the activities and in particular the public displays of piety of one of these organisations: the Hermandad de Nuestro Padre Jesús en la Columna ('Brotherhood of Our Father Jesus at the Column'), the foundation of which was given initial authorisation in about 1642 and confirmed some thirty years later.

The Cofradía de la Santa Vera Cruz was in a state of some crisis when the initiative of some of its members led to the establishment of the Hermandad de Nuestro Padre Jesús en la Columna, possibly in response to the threat of a fresh outbreak

---

[81] For a summary of the charitable activities of Priego's brotherhoods in the seventeenth century, see Alférez Molina, 117–28.

of plague, when the town council ordered and attended a special mass.[82] Following the formalisation of the Hermandad's foundation in 1673, there were an overwhelming number of requests for membership, although the number of brothers was strictly limited. The Cofradía de la Santa Vera Cruz and the Hermandad co-existed harmoniously as separate institutions, and the areas in which each would be expected to take the lead were clearly defined. It was only at the beginning of the nineteenth century that the Cofradía was to decline to the point that it was absorbed into the Hermandad.[83] On the other hand, there were obvious points of rivalry with the Hermandad del Nazareno, and these were to continue to exist far into the future. Both La Columna and El Nazareno were to have chapels constructed in close proximity to each other in the church of San Francisco, the former completed in 1679 (though with important later additions), and that of El Nazareno, a more elaborate Baroque creation, begun half a century later.

The constitution of the Hermandad de Jesús en la Columna is very clear and specific in setting out the responsibilities of its brothers, and this included the instructions for the procession on Jueves Santo (Maundy/Holy Thursday). There was an extensive tradition of such displays of devotion in Spain and particularly in Andalucía, and in Priego the spectacle of the Corpus Christi procession had already reached a height of splendour in the 1620s.[84] We have already seen how the veneration of fragments of the Holy Cross, carried in procession, had become a feature of the spiritual life of Priego, as in other towns of Andalucía, and how this had led to the establishment of the Cofradía de la Santa Vera Cruz in the mid-sixteenth century. However, now, a hundred years later, this procession was to be transformed into a 'Baroque spectacle' by the addition of *pasos* (platforms bearing

---

[82] Forcada Serrano, 2000, 55–56, emphasises the importance of fear of outbreaks of plague in the foundation of this and other such brotherhoods.
[83] Ibid., 85.
[84] Peláez Rosal and Rivas Carmona, 125.

sculptures related to the Crucifixion), rich decoration, participants in a variety of roles and a powerful musical element. This is essentially the form of the processions which has come down to us today.[85]

The constitution of the Hermandad describes in detail the Thursday evening procession, the most important of the three organised by the brotherhood in Holy Week, and from this a clear picture emerges of how that procession would have been made up by the late seventeenth century. A priest in the role of Jesus was accompanied by twelve brothers representing the apostles, followed by six more bearing the image of Jesus at the Column and eight carrying the *palio* or canopy. The remaining seventy-two brothers would be dressed in purple and wear a crown of thorns; in one hand they would carry a cross, with a skull under their arm, and in the other hand a scourge and their rosary; their legs would be bare and they would wear sandals, and round their waists and throats they would have cord made of esparto grass. The figure of Jesus would be preceded by the insignia of the brotherhood. The inventories of the brotherhoods' possessions, moreover, reveal that the combined procession of the Cofradía and the Columna grew steadily in complexity and splendour over the following decades, with the number of *pasos* increasing to four.[86]

---

[85] Forcada Serrano, 2000, 115. For a discussion of the significance of the term 'Baroque', see note 79.
[86] Ibid., 119–23.

Christ at the Column

This sculpture of the scene from Christ's passion was probably carved by the Granadan sculptor Alonso de Mena (1587–1646). It was commissioned as an object of devotion by the members of the Cofradía de la Vera Cruz ('Confraternity of the True Cross'), and its veneration was central to the foundation of the Hermandad de Nuestro Padre Jesús en la Columna ('Brotherhood of Our Father Jesus at the Column') in 1642. This sculpture occupies a prominent position in the procession that takes place each year on Holy Thursday. *Photograph by Antonio Jesús Villena.*

The Good Friday procession in Priego
The statue of Jesus of Nazareth ('El Nazareno') is carried through the town on Good Friday morning in the most dramatic part of Priego's Holy Week celebrations. It makes its way from its home in the church of San Francisco to the chapel of El Calvario, which stands on a height above the town. The procession is highly distinctive, with a large crowd of participants jostling to carry the statue.
Photograph by Antonio Jesús Villena.

Intimately associated with the Holy Thursday procession – although since the 1960s it has taken place on the Wednesday of Holy Week rather than the Thursday – is the *Prendimiento* or 'Arrest of Christ', a dramatic event which was to be performed before the beginning of the procession. This enactment of the Last Supper and the betrayal of Christ is described in detail in the initial constitution of the Hermandad de Jesús en la Columna. This sets out how the figure of Judas is to appear at the head of a 'squadron' of soldiers 'dressed in the manner of Jews', which he guides to the place where the Supper is taking place. By 1699, an agreement had been reached by which each of the existing brotherhoods was to contribute members to the *Escuadrón*. The wording in the Hermandad's constitution amounts to the clearest possible reminder of the guilt placed on the Jews and of why Judaism was considered to have no place in seventeenth-century Spanish society. It is not clear to what extent originally the members of the *Escuadrón* actually had the appearance of Jews or of Romans (or, indeed, of seventeenth-century Spanish soldiers), but there can be no doubt that the *sayones* or executioners, as they are still depicted in contemporary processions, are unequivocally represented as not only evil but also unmistakeably as Jews, wearing costumes (with their colourful conical hats) that associate them with penitents condemned by the Holy Inquisition.

A further important innovation associated with the Hermandad de la Columna were the May processions, which have continued until the present day to play a distinctive role in Priego's spiritual life. The May festival probably dates back to the initial period of the foundation of the Hermandad de la Columna in about 1642, and it was subsequently taken up by the brotherhoods of El Nazareno, La Soledad and El Buen Suceso. It was traditionally believed that it first took place in response to an imminent threat of plague, but it seems much more likely that its purpose was to put an end to a period of drought. Either way, its function was *rogativa*, that is to say, to obtain divine favour through a display of piety.[87] This festival, whose celebratory tone was in marked contrast with the more sombre Easter processions, was promoted and organised by the Hermandad de la Columna. Initially, it involved a novena (a series of nine masses), a sermon and an evening procession. The *cofradías* sought to endow the Eucharist with the greatest possible splendour, projecting the sacred function of the church out into

---

[87] Ibid., 155–58.

the street, and to this end, for example, the streets were strewn with sweet-smelling grasses. The festival grew steadily in importance and in splendour, both visually and in terms of its rich musical accompaniment, and by 1745 it included a spectacular firework display.

It is generally agreed that the May festival, involving impressive processions each Sunday in the month, is today the religious event most specifically associated with Priego. Moreover, although displays of popular piety similar to those that have just been described are characteristic of numerous Andalusian towns, it is beyond dispute that the role which the brotherhoods have continued to play in Priego – and their importance within the town's social fabric and in the creation of the community's collective beliefs and values – has been a highly distinctive one. Economically, the seventeenth century was a period of considerable economic difficulty both for Priego and for Spain as a whole, but from it there emerged structures and traditions which have continued to be a defining feature of the town into the twenty-first century.

*

The death in 1700 of the childless Carlos II, the last of Spain's Habsburg kings, led to a lengthy international conflict and the eventual installation on the Spanish throne of the Bourbon Felipe (Philippe) V, grandson of Louis XIV of France. He and his successors were to introduce sweeping reforms into their kingdom, reinforcing the centralising power of the monarchy and bringing about marked economic progress. In particular, the reign of Felipe's son Carlos III (1759–88) is generally accepted as marking a period of outstanding economic and administrative progress and of far-reaching social and cultural initiatives.

In Priego, the final years of the seventeenth century had already seen a degree of recovery in the town's financial affairs, resulting from good olive harvests at the beginning of the 1680s combined with effective administration of taxes, and by the end of the century the consequences of this were already evident in new projects such as the work done on the church of San Juan de Dios and the reconstruction of the old Fuente del Rey.[88] This was just the beginning, however, and the following century was to see increasing prosperity and a notable level of cultural achievement embodied in some of the town's most iconic artistic creations.

The early years of the eighteenth century were marked by the struggle for the throne of Spain known as La Guerra de Sucesión ('the War of the Spanish Succession'). This was an international conflict which pitted the defenders of Spain's new Bourbon monarchy – heavily dependent on French backing – against a 'grand alliance' of supporters of Archduke Charles, the Habsburg pretender to the throne, among whom the British and the Dutch played a major role. The capture of Gibraltar by the alliance in 1704 left the Madrid authorities fearing for the security of all Andalucía. The support for Felipe among the Spanish aristocracy was far from reliable, and Madrid itself fell into the hands of his enemies for a time. In 1705, Priego was required to contribute 183 troops to assist Cádiz. A further contingent was sent in the following year, and the people of the town were instructed to prepare to defend it against attack. In gratitude for its service to his cause, Felipe V was later to award Priego the title 'Most noble and loyal'.[89]

The spiritual concerns of the town continued to play a very prominent part in public life. In 1709, the town council met to discuss the serious problems by which it and the surrounding area were threatened: the effects of the war, famine, a plague of locusts and an infestation of insects attacking the holm oaks. As a result, the Virgin Mary in the form of 'la Purísima Concepción' (the Immaculate Conception) was adopted as *patrona perpetua* (or patron saint) of the town, alongside San Nicasio. Twenty years later, we find the council placing their trust in her to solve

---

[88] Peláez del Rosal and Rivas Carmona, 136–38.

[89] Ibid., 140–41.

a particularly vexing problem: the question of the sales tax known as the *alcabala* and the council's right to administer it and enjoy the income that it generated but which it had forfeited through falling seriously into arrears with its payments. This continued to cause serious difficulty to the town's authorities. In the council's minutes we find an agreement which included the stipulation that twenty-five masses were to be said for every year that the town authorities retained the right to collect the tax, and 300 *reales* were offered as a contribution towards the chapel being built for the Virgin in the church of San Francisco.[90]

The ploy was clearly not successful, however, for by 1753 the council was still without this critical source of income and so had at its disposal only two thirds of the funds that it required; and this amount was taken up by just three items: the doctor's salary, the costs of the Corpus Christi procession and those of maintaining a body of soldiers. In consequence, the town's authorities applied to extend temporary local taxes (such as those on the sale of taffeta and soap, wine brought into the town, the slaughter of livestock or the collection of acorns).[91] These taxes, known as *arbitrios*, were complicated and expensive to collect. Moreover, not only were the town's collective resources under severe strain but there is also evidence of continuing hardship endured by its people. There were a number of particularly bad years, resulting from either shortage of food or the spread of disease, such as 1738 when in the diocese of Córdoba 15,000 people are said to have died of starvation, or 1751 when there was an outbreak of smallpox.[92] In 1735, the council minutes tell us that the people of Priego were reduced to eating nothing but grass.[93]

---

[90] Peláez del Rosal (1960), 31–33; Peláez del Rosal and Rivas Carmona, 142–143. For the origins and the implications of the dispute over the *alcabala*, see above, Chapter 4.

[91] Peláez del Rosal and Rivas Carmona, 146–47.

[92] Durán Alcalá, 168–69.

[93] Forcada Serrano, 2000, 83.

The welfare of the people of Priego was certainly not helped by the continuing economic, judicial and administrative control exercised by the marquis of Priego (now also duke of Medinaceli), who, through his governor, had the right to make municipal appointments and to oversee the work of the officials. He also owned a significant proportion of the best agricultural land in the area around Priego and was the landlord of many of its people. Tenants were granted the right to build houses in the vicinity of the sources of water, and so settlements gradually sprang up. The marquisate gained more rent as a result but, while the amount of land did not increase, the number of people struggling to live off it grew. The result was increasing rural poverty, and the existence of such hardship among the poor and particularly the rural poor must not be forgotten as we contemplate Priego's considerable achievements during the second half of the eighteenth century.

Nevertheless, there were undoubtable important advances in the life of the town and its surrounding area. By the end of the eighteenth century, a third of the land within the *término* (or municipal area) of Priego was under some form of cultivation, although about half of this was planted with different kinds of oak tree (whose acorns were essential fodder for the pigs). About a tenth of the cultivated area was occupied by olive trees and about four times this amount was used for the production of cereal crops. Over the second half of the eighteenth century, there was a significant increase in the amount of olive oil produced, and at the end of that period 200 people are recorded as earning their living by tending livestock.[94]

In spite of the periodic bouts of serious hardship, the town's economic position had long since begun to improve, particularly as a result of the buoyancy of the silk industry.

---

[94] See Durán Alcalá, op. cit., 158–62, for a helpful survey of agriculture in the *término* of Priego in the period in question. The *término* is the area under the administration of the council of Priego and includes surrounding villages, of which at that time the largest were Almedinilla, Fuente-Tójar and Castil de Campos.

This had flourished in the area since being established by the *Moriscos*, on account of both the availability of cheap labour and the quality of their work, and their skills had clearly been passed on by the time of their expulsion. In the eighteenth century, the Bourbon monarchy's reformist policies provided a critical economic stimulus. In the mid-seventeenth century, there had already been some 4,000 mulberry trees in Priego's villages and in the area around the town, with another 800 in the urban area itself. Even more raw material was brought in from other parts of Spain and by now some 250 workers in Priego were involved in producing taffeta and smaller quantities of other silk-based textiles. These figures continued to increase steadily until, by the middle of the eighteenth century, some 15% of Priego's active population is known to have been working in the textile industry. The number of registered looms in the town increased steadily from 507 in 1684 to 1,160 in 1753. Production peaked between 1750 and 1780 when Priego occupied a prominent position among Andalucía's towns as an industrial centre.[95] This prosperity attracted immigrants from other parts of Spain, and Priego's population grew steadily from just under 9,000 in 1712 to 14,280 at the beginning of the following century.[96] Much of the silk-based fabric that was produced was exported, principally through the ports of Seville and Cádiz to America and Portugal. This was a luxury product which could command a high price. In addition, by the end of the eighteenth century, some 200 workers were employed in Priego in the production of goods made from flax, wool and hemp, and there was also a significant leather-working industry. The income generated by this industrial production was considerable, and this was to be reflected in various aspects of the town's evolution. Steady progress was made in the payment of the vast sum owed for the purchase of the *alcabalas,* and in spite of an

---

[95] Forcada Serrano, 2016, 18–23.

[96] Durán Alcalá, 168.

economic decline after 1780, by 1790, the council's minutes report the final elimination of what had long been a crippling debt.[97]

*

The eighteenth century was, without doubt, the most impressive period in Priego's history in terms of urban development and specifically with regard to the creation of a large body of ecclesiastical art and architecture of outstanding quality. All of this was made possible by a marked improvement in the town's finances, resulting initially from a series of good harvests in the late seventeenth century, a growth in trade and, above all, the huge success of the silk industry, which lasted until between 1780 and 1790.

Although Priego's population grew rapidly, the town did not extend beyond the already existing limits. Areas of agricultural land and previously unused spaces within the urban area were now used for building, as in the case of Calle Río, which was particularly affected by such intensive use of the land available. Already in the seventeenth century, stretches of the medieval town walls had been taken down and now numerous old buildings were demolished within what had been the walled area. For example, we know that in the first half of the eighteenth century, the Arch of la Encarnación, probably part of the old Gate of Santa Ana of Muslim Priego, was removed to make way for a private house. By this time, the arch was considered to be in a dangerous state.[98] In the now heavily overcrowded area of the Plaza del Llano, three houses were demolished and a sizeable space opened up to display to better effect the main doorway of the church of La Asunción, and over the course of the century a number of

---

[97] Peláez del Rosal and Rivas Carmona 152–54.

[98] Vera Aranda, 145; for the identification of this arch, see also Carmona Ávila, 2009, 197.

other changes were made in the layout of the Barrio de la Villa in order to accommodate the enlargement and enhancement of the town's principal church. In general, there was a concerted effort to improve the appearance and structure of the old town. Much greater attention was now being paid to the aesthetic qualities of the buildings, in keeping with the requirements of both a more prosperous aristocracy and, of course, the Church.[99]

Not only did the second half of the eighteenth century witness spectacular architectural achievement in the creation and elaboration of Priego's churches and convents but in addition this process determined the layout of the town, as its most important open spaces were often shaped to allow the best possible view of the buildings. In addition, it is important to bear in mind the extent to which, throughout the town, many small details serve to reinforce its relationship with Christian ritual:

> The town developed into a setting for Christian art which at the same time had the function of a liturgical ritual; this took the form of the Holy Week processions which turned the streets into sacred itineraries, embellishing them with alcoves and crosses heavy with religious symbolism in order to remind passers-by of their role as Christians and invite them to pray or meditate as they went on their way.[100]

---

[99] Vera Aranda 146–47.

[100] Alférez Molina, 165. These include, for example, numerous *hornacinas* (alcoves or niches) set into walls around the town. They contain images of Christ's suffering, in the form of statues or paintings, sometimes on tiles, relating to the themes of the Holy Week processions (ibid., 179–83).

Iglesia de Nuestra Señora de la Aurora

The original church on this site probably dates as far back as the fifteenth century, but the highly elaborate Baroque edifice with its overwhelmingly ornate interior and imposing façade was created in the second half of the eighteenth century by Juan de Dios Santaella. The façade seen here was completed in 1772 and is characterised by the use of polychromatic marble. *Photograph by Antonio Jesús Villena.*

As regards the artists who contributed so conspicuously to the creation of the town's rich heritage, it is possible to talk of a Priego 'school' of Baroque architecture, a group of individuals closely linked to Priego and the surrounding area. The first – and certainly one of the most influential of these – was the architect Francisco Hurtado Izquierdo (1669–1725), from Lucena. He worked in close collaboration with two brothers from Granada, Jerónimo and Teodosio Sánchez de Rueda, and later Teodosio's son and son-in-law, Marcos Sánchez de Rueda and Tomás Jerónimo Pedrajas. Jerónimo Sánchez de Rueda (1670–1749) worked on several of the most important artistic projects undertaken in Priego during his lifetime. Some of these were secular commissions, but principally they were for ecclesiastical buildings. They included altarpieces (*retablos*) and the chapel (or *camarín*) of the Immaculate Conception for the church of the convent of San Pedro; probably the chapel of the Cofradía de Jesús Nazareno in the church of San Francisco; and the remodelling of the church of La Asunción.[101] Among a second generation of artists, Juan de Dios Santaella (1718–82) was prolific in his output but is most famous for his work on the church of La Aurora (originally the *ermita* of San Nicasio) and on the elaborate doorway to the church of San Francisco. However, without doubt, the most spectacular creation of the Priego artists in the eighteenth century is the octagonal chapel of the *sagrario* (or sacrarium) of the church of La Asunción.[102] Decorated with a dazzling profusion of detail, it is generally considered to be an example of the rococo style at its best.[103] It was the work of a

---

[101] A *camarín* is a small chapel situated behind an altar, intended for the veneration of an image.

[102] The *sagrario* or sacrarium is a chapel which contains the tabernacle, holding the consecrated Eucharist.

[103] 'Rococo' in architecture, sculpture and the decorative arts is a style characterised by elegance, exuberant deoration and the extensive use of curving natural forms. It originated in France in about 1720 and the name is derived from the French word *rocaille*, which was applied to the shell-covered rock work used to decorate artificial grottoes.

native of Priego, Francisco Javier Pedrajas, and was begun in 1772 and completed in 1784. Pedrajas was another prolific and versatile artist whose other work included the final stages of the remodelling of the church of San Juan de Dios and the impressive *retablos* in the church of Las Mercedes.[104]

Altogether, in the second half of the eighteenth century, a large body of work of great quality was carried out on the churches of La Asunción, San Francisco, La Aurora, San Marcos, San Pedro, Santa Clara, El Calvario, San Juan de Dios, Las Angustias, Las Mercedes, Nuestra Señora del Carmen, La Virgen de la Cabeza and La Virgen del Calvario. The whole process took place over more than a century, but the period of most intense activity was from 1750 to 1790, with its high point at about 1770.[105] This extraordinary programme of new building, reconstruction, elaboration and embellishment, carried out in a style that reflected an overall coherence and sense of common purpose, constitutes an unmistakeable statement about the identity and character of Priego's community. It is a demonstration of the wealth and prosperity generated by the town's industrial success but also of its devotion to the values of the Catholic Church, clearly expressed in the influence exercised by the *cofradías*.[106]

---

[104] For a succinct introduction to the life and work of some of these artists, see the articles in the *Diccionario Biográfico Español* published by the Real Academia de la Historia (available online): by Mª de los Ángeles Raya Raya on Francisco Hurtado Izquierdo, Jerónimo Sánchez de Rueda, Francisco Javier Pedrajas and Remigio del Mármol, and by Manuel Peláez del Rosal on Juan de Dios Santaella. It must also be borne in mind that these artists did not work alone but were supported by substantial teams of craftsmen.

[105] Vera Aranda, 145.

[106] Forcada Serrano, 1992, 26–27, cites a revealing example of how, even in times of relative financial difficulty, a *cofradía* (that of la Virgen de las Mercedes) managed to find the resources necessary to ensure the completion of a project by organising a series of six bullfights.

The chapel of the *sagrario* (or sacrarium) of the church of La Asunción
Originally built in the first half of the sixteenth century, La Asunción was remodelled in the late eighteenth century. The sacrarium, the most dazzling achievement of Priego's Baroque artists, was begun in 1772 and completed in 1784. It was principally the work of a native of Priego, Francisco Javier Pedrajas. *Photograph by Antonio Jesús Villena.*

It is worth noting, however, that in important respects this building ran counter to the ideas of the Enlightenment, which by the second half of the eighteenth century dominated the ideas of politicians and intellectuals in the court and the administration of Spain's Bourbon monarchs.[107] Not only did this lead to a determination to reduce the influence and power of the Church, which was argued to be in part responsible for poverty and

---

[107] The Enlightenment was an intellectual and philosophical movement which originated in the late seventeenth century and became dominant in Europe in the eighteenth century. It emphasised the importance of reason, individualism and religious tolerance, and it opposed the fixed dogmas of the Church.

backwardness in much of the country, but there was also pressure for broader social and cultural change, including in attitudes to the arts. In Madrid, from 1777, the Academia de Bellas Artes de San Fernando effectively made neoclassicism the official style for all works being produced, only giving permission for work to proceed if it conformed to its norms.[108] This made no difference at all to the work being done in Priego. Nevertheless, it is interesting to read the judgement on the sagrarium expressed by the liberal and anticlerical politician and writer Pedro Alcalá-Zamora: 'The sculpture of the *sagrario* is solid even though it does not conform to the architectural regulations, and, although overladen with carved decoration and white plaster reliefs, altogether it forms a pleasing and magnificent whole.'[109]

Of course, not all the construction which took place in Priego during the eighteenth century was of ecclesiastical buildings. For example, a certain amount of rebuilding was made necessary by the damage done in 1755 by the notorious earthquake that devastated Lisbon. This included the construction of a new arcade in the square by the Puerta del Agua (now the Plaza de Andalucía, situated at the top of Calle Ribera) and the restoration of several houses belonging to members of the nobility and also the Colegio de la Asunción.

Most notably, working right at the beginning of the nineteenth century but still in the Baroque style, Remigio del Mármol was responsible for the design of the most important secular creation associated with the 'Priego School'. The monumental Fuente del Rey ('King's Fountain') consisted of three pools with a total of 139 spouts and was dominated by the figures of Poseidon (Neptune) and his wife, Amphitrite, goddess of the sea. It lies just below the original fountain, which had been constructed in the sixteenth century and later acquired the name of the Fuente

---

[108] Forcada Serrano, 2000, 191.

[109] Alcalá-Zamora, 11. The existing edition of this short study does not, in fact, have printed page numbers.

de la Salud (it was dedicated to la Virgen de la Salud – 'the Virgin of Health') on account of what were believed to be its life-saving properties during times of plague.[110] The first pool of the new fountain in fact dates from the early seventeenth century, but the striking creation of the early eighteenth century was much more elaborate and unmistakeably consistent with the Baroque style that is characteristic of Priego's artistic heritage as a whole.

One other feature of the Fuente del Rey does, however, require special mention. The first of its series of three fountains contains a sculpture of a lion fighting with a serpent, and this is generally accepted to be an early work by José Álvarez Cubero. This distinguished figure was born in Priego and was the godson of Francisco Javier Pedrajas, but he was destined to become known internationally as a neoclassical sculptor.[111] The age of Baroque splendour in Priego was finally approaching its end.

---

[110] Alférez Molina, 161.

[111] Neoclassicism, an artistic movement which coincided with the Age of Enlightenment, emphasises the principles of simplicity and symmetry. It represents a marked shift away from the exuberance of rococo.

Priego de Córdoba at the beginning of the nineteenth century

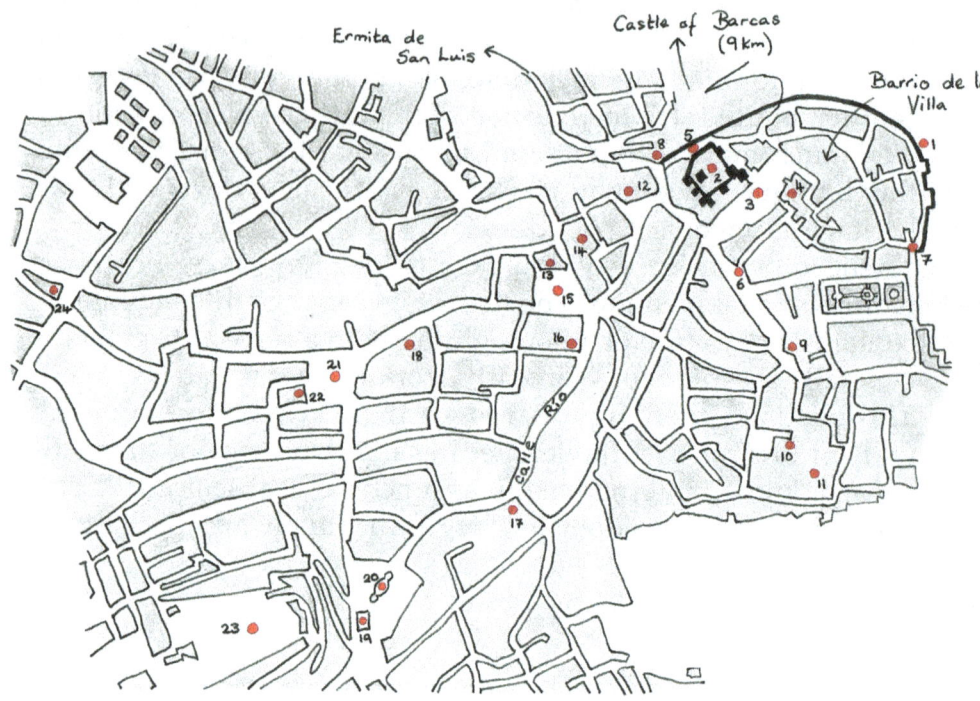

1. Tajo del Adarve: escarpment
2. Alcazaba: castle
3. Plaza de los Escribanos (also known as Plaza del Llano and Llano de la Iglesia)
4. Iglesia de Nuestra Señora de la Asunción
5. Arco de San Bernardo
6. Puerta de Santa Ana
7. Puerta del Sol
8. Carnicerías Reales: municipal meat market and slaughterhouse
9. Iglesia de la Aurora
10. Iglesia de San Francisco
11. Franciscan Convent of San Esteban
12. Iglesia de San Pedro Apóstol
13. Convent of San Antonio (also known as Santa Clara)
14. Convent-Hospital of San Juan de Díos (previously known as San Onofre)
15. Plaza de la Constitución
16. Iglesia de Nuestra Señora de las Angustias
17. Iglesia de Nuestra Señora del Carmen
18. Iglesia de las Mercedes
19. Fuente de la Salud
20. Fuente del Rey
21. El Palenque
22. El Pósito: granary and grain market
23. Ermita del Calvario
24. Ermita de San Marcos

Plaza: Square
Iglesia: Church
Arco: Arch
Puerta: Gate
Fuente: Spring, fountain
Ermita: Chapel

La Fuente del Rey ('the King's Fountain')
This elaborate Baroque creation was designed by Remigio del Mármol (born in nearby Alcalá la Real) and was completed in 1803. It is famed for its 139 spouts, many of them emerging from extravagantly fashioned faces, and the central feature is a sculpture of Neptune and the sea nymph Amphitrite in a chariot drawn by horses which appear to emerge from beneath the water. In the background is the older fountain known as the Fuente de la Salud. *Photograph by Antonio Jesús Villena.*

CHAPTER 6

Poverty and Prosperity, Reform and Reaction

༄

I: Crisis and conflict

The prosperity which had underpinned Priego's spectacular wave of creativity was not to last. Pedro Alcalá-Zamora, soldier, politician and scholar, writing in the final years of the eighteenth century, gives a succinct explanation of the difficulty which now confronted the town:

> Around the year 1780 the production [of silk] suddenly declined. In just a few years the precarious wellbeing of the people of Priego disappeared completely, to the extent that there no longer exist either the machinery or people who can operate it. Two or three looms are all that remain and during the periods that they are in use it is with silk from elsewhere that is sent to the people here to be worked.[112]

Within twenty years, 80% of the area's mulberry trees had been uprooted, and by 1850, with the exception of a very small number of looms, the industry that had driven the town's wave of prosperity had entirely ceased to exist. What had led to such a severe and rapid decline? Principally, it seems, it was the increasingly unreliable quality of the work now being done, partly as a result of the involvement of the marquises of Priego who dispensed with the necessary quality controls in order to

---

[112] Alcalá-Zamora, 9. See also Forcada Serrano, 2016, 24–30, for a fuller explanation of the decline of Priego's silk industry and its implications.

increase their own profit.[113] However, the manufacturers also proved unable to adjust to the production of new kinds of materials, and in addition considerable difficulty was caused by the increase in import taxes in Portugal and Portuguese America and by competition from cheaper textiles, notably English cotton goods. The consequences were dramatic. If Alcalá-Zamora's criticism of the physical and moral damage done to the people of Priego is bitter, the report on the area by the geographer Tomás López, written some twenty years earlier, makes even grimmer reading. As a result of the ruin of the textile industry, essentially through mismanagement and greed, many families had been forced to leave in order to seek work in the factories of Granada, Málaga, Córdoba and Sevilla …

> It is pitiful to see … so great a legion of beggars of all ages and sexes presenting so sad a spectacle, in the nakedness and wretchedness of the multitude of paupers begging for alms every day; for they have the look of walking corpses. These were people who but a short time ago were known for their decency, application and love of work, but this work has run out and it will be necessary either for them to depart for good or to perish, if some rapid solution is not put in place.[114]

López is extremely careful not to level any criticism directly at the marquises themselves, but he has strong words for their subordinates, whom he considers responsible for serious abuses. He lists several of these abuses, including the prevention – without legal right or justification – of the installation of mills, bakers' ovens or taverns, all of this under the jurisdiction of the mayor, who had been appointed by the marquis. In the light of such criticisms, it is not difficult to see why the nineteenth-century liberals were intent on putting an end to the feudal authority of the aristocracy.

---

[113] Alcalá-Zamora, 10. He is scathing in his criticism of both the marquisate and of the 'sycophantic' town council for allowing this to happen.
[114] Tomás López, 341–42.

*

For the Spanish people as a whole, the end of the eighteenth century and the early decades of the nineteenth century were a troubled time which saw economic progress paralysed. With regard to Priego itself, the historian Miguel Forcada describes the entire period of 1803–43 as 'without any qualification, a negative period in the town's life'.[115]

The reign of Carlos IV (1788–1808) witnessed an extended period of crisis which culminated in the entry into Spain of the Napoleonic armies. After a sustained conflict known in English as the Peninsular War but in Spanish as the War of Independence, the Bourbon monarchy was restored in the person of Fernando VII, whose reign of almost twenty years was marked by a lengthy struggle between liberals and absolutists.

It has been argued that '[m]uch of modern Spanish history is explained by the imposition of "advanced" liberal institutions on an economically and socially "backward" and conservative society'.[116] We shall see these forces at work in the development of Priego, too. In the conflict between 'liberal' and 'absolutist' elements, attitudes to the Church constituted one of the most contentious issues.[117] Given what we have already seen of the nature of Priego's origins and history, it is easy to understand why the religious question was to be of such fundamental importance over the following decades in determining the town's response to the constantly shifting picture at a national level.

The national political crisis which began with the abdication of Carlos IV in 1808 was reflected in events in Priego. The initial reaction, as elsewhere in Spain, was one of rejoicing, and the

---

[115] Forcada Serrano, 2000, 190.

[116] Raymond Carr, 1980, 1.

[117] An 'absolutist' theory of government implied the existence of unlimited, centralised authority vested in the monarch, whose power was not held in check by any judicial, legislative or electoral body.

announcement of Fernando VII's accession to the throne was celebrated by a variety of public festivities. The country's invasion by French troops, however, brought about a dramatic change of mood, and on 29th May – four weeks after the popular uprising and subsequent acts of repression by the French in the capital – Priego's council determined to join the national campaign of resistance and began to recruit troops and raise a subscription towards the cost of the war. In early June, the French army occupied and sacked Córdoba but then took the easier route towards Alcaudete, leaving Priego untouched. On 19th July, a unit of troops from Priego, commanded by Captain Pedro Alcalá-Zamora, took part in the battle of Bailén, fought some 80 kilometres north-east of Priego, which ended in a famous victory for the Spanish forces. In Priego, there were joyous celebrations, and the town paid tribute to its returning troops.

Militia companies were formed, but they appear to have been able to offer little resistance when, by the beginning of 1810, the French army returned and captured Priego. Over the following two years, a unit of French troops remained garrisoned in the town, based in the convent of San Francisco. During that time, there is no record of any meetings of the town council, and religious events were largely suppressed. The economic cost to the community was considerable, as the town bore the burden of an occupying force as well as that of contributing a substantial sum to the Spanish army, which was sustaining a bitter guerrilla war.[118]

By the end of 1813, an alliance of British, Spanish and Portuguese forces had driven the French armies from the Peninsula. With its economic fabric seriously damaged by the war, Spain was entering a period of social and political instability, although it had been on a note of optimism that in 1812 the country's new liberal constitution had been approved by the *Cortes* (Parliament), which gathered in Cádiz. This highly

---

[118] Peláez del Rosal and Rivas Carmona, 166–67.

significant document, although it emphasised the position of Roman Catholicism as Spain's official and sole religion, introduced a wide range of liberal reforms, emphasising the freedoms and rights of the people and removing feudal privileges. In Priego, it was celebrated enthusiastically by a large crowd gathered on the Llano de la Iglesia, which was now to be known as the Plaza de la Constitución. '¡Viva la religión! ¡Viva la Patria! ¡Viva el Rey!' ('Long live religion! Long live the Homeland! Long live the King!') was the cry that went up.[119] A bust of Fernando VII was commissioned from Remigio del Mármol to be placed by the Fuente del Rey next to a plaque commemorating the Constitution and, a few days later, in the presence of the abbot of Alcalá la Real, representatives of the Church swore to follow and respect the principles that it embodied. From 1813, the Franciscans were able to return to the convent of San Esteban (or San Francisco), from which they had been expelled during the period of French occupation.

The harmony was not to last. It was not long before reprisals started in Priego against those who had collaborated with the French. Moreover, just two years later, in 1814, the Cádiz Constitution was repealed, returning Fernando VII to the status of an absolute monarch.[120] The town council, which had been formed in accordance with the Constitution, was now dissolved, and the one that had existed before the entry of the French into Spain in 1808 was restored. The duke of Medinaceli (the marquis of Priego) now regained the right to make appointments to municipal positions. Priego, like most of Spain, was embarking on a long period of confrontation between those who sought to reform or abolish the features of the old absolutist regime and on the other hand its supporters, implacably opposed to change.[121]

---

[119] Ibid., 168.

[120] It is ironic that Fernando, nicknamed 'El Deseado' ('Longed for'), who had been the embodiment of his people's hopes for the future, turned out to be one of Spain's most notoriously reactionary monarchs.

[121] See Forcada Serrano, 1997, 180–81.

1820 saw another change of direction, when a military uprising led by Rafael del Riego forced King Fernando to return to an acceptance of the 1812 Constitution, thus ushering in what came to be known as the Liberal Triennium. Priests were obliged to explain the meaning of the Constitution to their flocks as part of the Sunday Mass. In Priego, a Liberal council was rapidly formed, which sought to introduce a range of measures concerned with public works and with education (notably in connection with the girls' school run by the lay community of Nuestra Señora de las Angustias). Once again, the friars were expelled from the convent of San Francisco. There was also a further attempt by the *síndico* José Tomás to put an end to the town's feudal relationship with the dukes of Medinaceli.[122] There was no time for any proposed reforms to bear fruit, however, for in 1823 a French army, sponsored by the principal European powers, invaded Spain and once again restored absolute rule. The reforming measures of the previous three years were promptly reversed.

Nationally, monastic orders had been suppressed and most of the possessions of religious organisations (including those of the *cofradías*) had been declared state property. On the other hand, it seems that in Priego the impact of the various decrees aimed at ecclesiastical institutions had been relatively slight and that here the *cofradías* had been carrying on their activities largely unhindered.[123] In this respect, Miguel Forcada makes a very significant point:

> The presence of members of the Alcalá-Zamora family during this period among the brothers of the 'Columna' – as well as other notable 'enlightened' and liberal members of the Priego community – offers a further explanation for why in Priego, right up to the present day, the traditions of the *cofradías* have remained so much alive: not only were the *hermandades* defended by the conservative elements in society but in addition people of a

---

[122] A *síndico* was an elected representative of the people.
[123] Forcada Serrano, 2000, 204.

liberal and progressive outlook saw no contradiction – or took this for granted as a human characteristic – in collaborating in and even directing the activities of such bodies. ... One of the most prominent figures in the Council which governed Priego during the Liberal Triennium was the elected representative José Fernando Berdugo, who was given the responsibility for finance, fiestas and schools and was one of those involved in drawing up the programme of modernisation produced by that Council. Well, this highly prominent member of the liberal establishment was a brother of the 'Columna'.[124]

Although Priego saw no open conflict during this troubled period of Fernando's reign, a highly dangerous incident was narrowly avoided in September 1823: a skirmish between the troops of General Riego, continuing his struggle against a king that he saw as despotic and incompetent, and those of General Francisco Ballesteros. Ballesteros had established his headquarters near Priego, where the army's General Military Hospital was temporarily installed in the convent of San Francisco. There was no serious confrontation between the two armies, but Riego entered Priego, seized several members of the town council and threatened to sack the town if his demands for money and supplies were not met. After receiving a substantial sum raised by the citizens, he and his army departed, only to be decisively defeated by a royalist army near Jaén three days later.

With the defeat and death of General Riego, Spain's 'liberal dream' came to an end. With hindsight, the brutal significance of the event is clear: 'Really what was re-established for ten years was the implacable persecution of everything that smacked of liberalism, with a new period of despotic, intransigent and inept government which extended far beyond [Fernando's] first period as an absolute monarch.'[125] In Priego, however, the new mayor, a supporter of the repressive new regime, viewed matters from a very different angle when he praised the way in

---

[124] Ibid., 205.

[125] Isidoro Lara Martín-Portugués, 28.

which the town had at all times remained loyal to the king, holding off the 'cowardly revolutionary armies'.[126] In 1824, Field Marshal Juan Nepomuceno Prats went further when he spoke of the town's achievement:

> Throughout the province and even the whole Peninsula, there is common knowledge of the spirit of loyalty to the king which has always been predominant in Priego. Just as well known are the innumerable sacrifices which its determined citizens have made on His Majesty's behalf. Their indomitable bravery would be difficult to surpass, for they faced up to the gravest of dangers at a time when, with the town surrounded by enemy armies which menaced it on all sides, its heroes needed all of their courage in order to cope with such overwhelming threats. The citizens alone had to rely on just their limited resources and their hope. They would have been ready, had they been attacked by the enemy, to risk their lives.[127]

If during the period of liberal dominance there had been persecution in Priego of prominent supporters of the monarchy, with the return to absolutism the situation was reversed. In 1814, Pedro Alcalá-Zamora had been forced to flee to France on account of his liberal views. Now he once again found himself out of favour. Accused of disloyalty and of freemasonry, he was sentenced to eighteen months' imprisonment and exiled to Granada.[128] Fines were imposed for speaking out against the rights of the Church. Indeed, so great was the pro-royalist sentiment in the town that its citizens pressed for the re-establishment of the Inquisition 'in support of absolute monarchy and religion'.[129]

In terms of its economic development, Priego was at a low

---

[126] Forcada Serrano, 1997, 181.

[127] Peláez del Rosal and Rivas Carmona, 172.

[128] See the article by Peláez del Rosal in the Real Academia de la Historia's *Diccionario biográfico*.

[129] Peláez Rosal and Rivas Carmona, 173.

point during this troubled period, with its population shrinking, particularly in the urban area. A combination of the sharp decline in the silk industry (literally non-existent by 1826), a series of poor harvests, a number of epidemics and the consequences of war left the town desperately poor. In 1834, for example, cholera raged through several of Priego's villages: Almedinilla, Sileras, Zamoranos, El Cañuelo, Castil de Campos, Fuente-Tójar, Esparragal and Zagrilla.

In 1817–18, a serious drought made irrigation impossible and the water mills could not function. There was no money for construction, and the physical collapse of Priego's municipal buildings left the council with no base of its own. It remained peripatetic, forced to rent premises. A report which it submitted to Córdoba in 1827 describes the state of extreme poverty to which the agricultural workers had been reduced and the paralysis of trade. In the following year, an epidemic was to cause the death of 500 children. Formal education hardly existed, with just three teachers in the entire area.[130]

II: Reform and revolution

Fernando VII died in 1833 and was succeeded by his three-year-old daughter, Isabel. Initially, it was her mother, María Cristina, who acted as regent, and the remainder of the decade was marked by a civil war between their liberal supporters and those of Fernando's brother, Carlos María Isidro, who was quick to lay claim to the throne and attracted the backing of the most radical proponents of absolutism. Carlos was to give his name to a right-wing political movement which has lasted until the present day and to a series of conflicts which repeatedly troubled nineteenth-century Spain. The so-called First Carlist War, which lasted from 1833 to 1840, was the most

---

[130] For this dire picture of the state to which Priego had been reduced, see Forcada Serrano, 1997, 182–83.

extreme manifestation of the confrontation between liberal and absolutist beliefs, and it was to endure for most of Isabel's long reign. Priego itself epitomised these divisions, though, fortunately, it escaped violent conflict. For almost half a century it was to stand out as one of the Andalusian towns which contained a conspicuous element identifying with Carlism and its reactionary values, while at the same time there continued to be strong support in the town for the liberal constitution and for the opponents of absolutism.

Indeed, in the opening years of the new liberal regime, it was the popular movement for reform that was to the fore. Pedro Alcalá-Zamora was elected to the national parliament, the *Cortes*. He is a figure deserving of special mention for his many-sided role in Priego's history: in his various capacities of soldier, politician and writer on the development of the town and its economy, in the course of his lengthy and colourful career, he made a massive contribution as a defender of liberal and progressive ideas.

In August 1835, a popular demonstration in Priego demanded the inclusion of the word 'Constitution' in the name of the square outside the council chambers (a demand which was promptly conceded) and also the closure of the convents and the dismissal or expulsion from the town of a range of individuals associated with Carlist ideology. It was not long before all Church representatives were suspended from their positions of responsibility on the orders of the civil governor of the province.

Nationally, the implementation of the radical policy of *desamortización* (disentailment) was at the centre of the political and economic strategy of the new liberal government. This far-reaching programme of reform was promulgated by Juan Álvarez de Mendizábal, who for a short time in 1835–36 served as prime minister. The policy had a short-term financial objective, notably that of raising money to pay for the cost of the Carlist war, but there were also broader long-term aims. Until now, the vast estates which belonged to the Church, to the nobility and to some towns had continued to be attached firmly to their owners. There was no chance of such property being divided up or removed from their possession, and so it was seen as bringing no benefit to the nation as a whole. The solution to this seemed to liberal economists to lie in a process of privatisation and agricultural reform which would put an end to the chronic unemployment of landless farm workers. Disentailment was supported by anti-clerical elements of the government but also resulted from a desire to exploit underused land and property by contributing to the creation of a tax-paying landed middle class. A key element of the programme of reform was the expropriation – without compensation – of ecclesiastical properties, which were to be sold off at auction. This was followed in 1835 by further legislation which authorised the sale of the rural property held by town councils, by the state and by religious bodies including military Orders and *cofradías*. In Priego, before the end of the year, the friars had already been expelled from the convents of both San Pedro and San Francisco (for the third time, but on this occasion definitively). In 1845, the convent of San Francisco was sold off in a public auction and in the decades that ensued, among its various uses, it was to serve as the home of factories – first for pottery and later for textiles – before eventually falling into almost total ruin.[131]

The programme of disentailment sought to inject more money into the national economy. However, its success in this respect was at best limited, and it in fact had a number of negative consequences, including those of depriving the Church of resources on which it relied for its traditional care-related tasks and of seriously harming the country's artistic heritage. It also led to the concentration of agricultural resources in the hands of an oligarchy of nobles, landowners, members of the middle classes and speculators who failed to invest their wealth to the benefit of the landless poor. In the long term, in the Priego area as throughout much of Andalucía, the result was to reinforce

---

[131] For a concise history of the convent of San Francisco, see Peláez del Rosal, 2014, 5–9.

economic and social divisions and ultimately to contribute to the growing lack of political stability.

On the other hand, one other reform, introduced by the liberal administration in 1837, was to have particular implications for Priego. This was the abolition – this time successful and definitive – of seignorial jurisdiction (*señoríos*), which meant the removal of the essentially feudal control which the House of Aguilar, the Marquisate of Priego and the Duchy of Medinaceli had held over the town over the past three centuries.

In September 1836, a group of Priego citizens joined the National Militia in Córdoba to take part in the ultimately unsuccessful defence of the city against the Carlist general Gómez Damas. It was probably as an act of retaliation against their action that within a month a Carlist force, including volunteers from Priego and nearby Carcabuey, had launched an attack on Priego itself, sacking houses and committing atrocities in some of the outlying streets. The community now prepared to defend itself against a more serious attack but this never came, although there was continuing friction between Carlists and the dominant liberals. In the following years, the town walls were repaired and the number of points of access restricted. In 1837, the promulgation of the new liberal Constitution (essentially a revised version of that of 1812) was celebrated with a variety of festivities, which included dancing in what had been the convent of San Francisco. Three years later, as tensions heightened nationally, Priego's council stood up against the conservative authorities in Córdoba in spite of threats and outright hostility and gave its support to General Espartero's military declaration in Madrid in favour of the Constitution. Several prominent opponents of the constitutional government were then exiled from Priego. A measure which was representative of the council's standpoint, although it was only to prove of relatively short duration, was the renaming of several streets: for example, Calle Carrera de las Monjas ('Street of the Nuns', so named because of its proximity to the Clarist convent) became Calle de La Libertad ('Street of Liberty'), while the Fuente del Rey was now the Fuente del Triunfo ('Fountain of Triumph').

With Isabel II ruling in her own right from 1843, political events both nationally and locally entered a more stable phase, although the Carlist presence in Priego remained prominent. Such figures as General Manuel López Caracuel, a native of the town who returned in 1863 from a period of exile, would continue to be a focus for Carlist support. At the other end of the political spectrum, as the end of Isabel's reign approached, the priest Luis Alcalá-Zamora was to come to the fore as a proponent of liberal revolution.

The people of Priego – the town and its surrounding territory – continued to endure periods of serious poverty. Although there was rich and fertile land, there were also quite extensive areas which were unproductive. A study dating from the second half of the 1840s continued to contrast the heady days of the eighteenth century with the current lack of industry and commerce: just two silk looms were functioning, while trade was limited to the export of oil and grain (principally to Málaga) and some fruit (to Granada).[132] The council minutes for 1847 report a demonstration by agricultural workers clamouring for assistance.[133] There was large-scale emigration in search of work, notably to the cities of Granada and Málaga. In 1843–44, the three largest villages in the municipal area, Almedinilla, Fuente-Tójar and Castil de Campos, were given autonomous status, and in the case of the first two (and to a limited extent the third) this has been retained until the present day. In 1867, there was a serious drought, and so great was the need for the distribution of food that it came to be known as 'el año de la sopa' ('the year of soup').

In a survey of the town's facilities produced in the 1840s there are some signs of the development of basic social amenities: for example, the school that had been established after the

---

[132] See Madoz, 213–16.

[133] Forcada Serrano, 1997, 186.

expulsion of the friars, in the convent of San Pedro, as well as one other school, with a total of three teachers and attended by some 200 boys. There was also a school for girls, which had been founded in 1787 under the auspices of Nuestra Señora de las Angustias (though it was commented that the teaching on offer there 'could be improved'). It is perhaps surprising to see that in 1841 a theatre was established in the town by a society of thirty-five landowners and businessmen.[134] On the whole, however, the picture which emerges is one of a community with very limited means existing amidst the memories of past glories. Educational provision was indeed lamentable: in 1835, in Priego itself, only 5% of men and boys could read and write and 2% of women and girls, and in most of the surrounding area the figures were lower still. Throughout the century, little was done to remedy the situation, with progress severely limited by the lack of suitable premises, resources and any real commitment to change on the part of the municipal authorities.[135]

*

In 1868, the conflict embodied in the successful national uprising against Isabel II was reflected in disturbances in Priego. These led to the resignation of the mayor and the establishment of a revolutionary committee headed by Gregorio Alcalá-Zamora y Caracuel, who promptly appointed a new town council. In due course, the promulgation of another new constitution was accompanied by enthusiastic celebrations. Serious confrontations were avoided.

One of the council's initial measures was to commandeer the Clarist convent of San Antonio (which stood in the centre of the town on the site of the present town hall). The justification in the eyes of the Madrid government for such seizures was clear ('Considering that these religious communities formed an

---

[134] Madoz, 214–15.
[135] Ruiz-Burruecos, 69–76.

integral and important part of the shameful and oppressive regime which the nation has just brought down in such a glorious fashion ...').[136] The building served as a barracks for the National Militia but was soon demolished to make way for a food market. It is not surprising that the nearby Calle Carrera de las Monjas was, temporarily at least, renamed Calle Prim (after the liberal general and architect of the 1868 revolution).

Six years of complex political manoeuvrings on the national stage – including the troubled period of the First Republic – were to pass before the re-establishment of the Bourbon monarchy in the person of King Alfonso XII in December 1874. However, throughout this dangerous period, Priego was to remain largely free of serious conflict. Juan Calvo Moreno, provincial representative for the district, was particularly successful in helping the town through the political labyrinth. It is revealing, in view of all the anti-clerical pressures, that in Priego the *cofradías* were able to carry on with their activities practically unhindered. During these six years, hardly any processions took place in Córdoba and most other towns in the province, but in Priego not only were these events organised without any problems but the May fiestas actually now acquired 'a great splendour'.[137]

In spite of further acts of reprisal in the town against the Carlists, their leading figure in Priego, General Caracuel (not to be confused with the liberal Gregorio Alcalá-Zamora y Caracuel), was dissuaded from leading an uprising in the town and left to take part in the conflict in the north of Spain. Still, Priego continued to be seen as a home to one of Andalucía's most committed groups of Carlists and in June 1874 the government sent a unit of fifty troops to the town, where they remained throughout the summer. However, in due course, with the eventual defeat of the Carlist forces nationally and the disappearance (for the foreseeable future) of the movement from

---

[136] Peláez del Rosal, 2006, 631.

[137] Forcada Serrano, 2000, 265.

the Spanish scene, a group of prominent Carlists appeared before the Priego town council to confirm their decision to submit definitively to the authority of the government and recognise the constitutional monarchy of King Alfonso. The resulting political situation in Priego is neatly summed up by Manuel López Calvo:

> In conclusion, it can be observed that as the democratic experience came to an end there remained a core of radical democrats, represented by the Alcalá-Zamora family, but also that the town of Priego lived through the revolutionary process in a state of relative apathy, without any excessive politicisation such as that which occurred among the popular urban classes or the groups of agricultural workers in several towns situated in the Cordoban *campiña*.[138] On the other hand, the extremist conservative elements were unable to increase their social and political influence, with the town remaining under government control, whatever that government might be. For this rural society, one of the longest periods of stability in Spain's history was about to begin.[139]

III: Years of stability

Nationally – and locally – the system of two parties, Liberal and Conservative, was made to work by a sophisticated system of vote rigging. This had originated in the 1840s. The so-called *turno pacífico* (peaceful alternation in power) operated through a range of fraudulent activities, combined with patronage and intimidation, with a local authority figure (*cacique*) as its key element. This allowed the Ministry of the Interior in Madrid to exercise very close control over the composition of the national *Cortes*. It was corrupt, but it worked. In Priego, one particularly influential

---

[138] The *campiña cordobesa* is an extensive area of largely agricultural land which stretches south from the Guadalquivir's flood plain as far as the edge of the hills of the Subbética.
[139] López Calvo, 29.

individual who represented the district on behalf of the Liberal party was Juan Manuel Sánchez y Gutiérrez de Castro, Duke of Almodóvar (elected in 1879 and 1881), and in 1881 he was responsible for the town (or *villa*) of Priego being granted the honorific title of *ciudad* in recognition of its 'constant support for the Constitutional Monarchy'. Another key figure who rose to prominence during this period was Carlos Valverde López, a wealthy farmer and landowner but also distinguished both by his work as a poet, dramatist and novelist and by his achievement as a politician (mayor of Priego from 1890 to 1893 and elected as a conservative member of the *Cortes* in 1896). From 1905, the liberal faction was once again to be dominant, and the preeminent individual on both local and national levels would be Niceto Alcalá-Zamora. Over the following decades, the rivalry between the Valverde and Alcalá-Zamora families was to leave a deep mark on political and social developments in Priego.

The period of peace and relative political and social harmony which followed the restoration of the monarchy in 1875 was to see a dramatic upturn in Priego's economic fortunes. This must, however, be set against a panorama of immense social divisions, notably between the wealthy landowning class and, at the other end of the scale, the landless agricultural workers known as *jornaleros*. These were hired by the day and were immensely vulnerable at times of shortage, such as those resulting from periods of drought or extended bad weather.[140] There were major natural disasters, too. In 1885, a serious earthquake (followed by several aftershocks) shook the area, killing two people and bringing down much of the roof of the church of El Carmen, and in the same year there were torrential rainstorms followed by an outbreak of cholera, which killed 2,500 people in Jaén and threatened Priego. The *cofradías* organised special masses to plead for divine protection, as indeed they did once again in 1891 as a result of the drought.[141]

---

[140] Ibid., 65–76: López Calvo paints a stark picture of the prevailing economic divisions and their consequences.

[141] Forcada Serrano, 2000, 313–14.

Economically, Priego and the surrounding area had stagnated. A report submitted by its mayor to the provincial administration in 1862 recognised the immense importance of re-establishing the town's industrial role: it had fallen back on agriculture for its income and, although undoubted progress had been made in exploiting land previously unsuited for cultivation, if a suitable level of prosperity was to be achieved, rapid industrial progress was vital. The rivers and the water mills were a valuable asset, but it was evident that above all it was necessary for there to be a marked improvement in the means for communication by road and – if possible – for the establishment of links by rail.[142]

From the 1860s, however, there is evidence of the production in Priego of textiles combining silk and cotton, and by the end of the following decade several companies in the town were producing cotton textiles. Output increased markedly as a result of the introduction of the new Jacquard loom and gradually the sector began to make a significant contribution to the economic development of the community. This progress was accompanied by a rapid increase in the production of olive oil, which had been boosted by the extensive planting of olive trees on land previously considered inappropriate. In 1906, there were twenty-six olive oil mills in Priego, as well as nine textile mills (and seven hat makers). Priego's oil began to win prizes in international competitions, and it was now possible to invest part of the profits from the export of oil in the further development of the silk industry.[143] Another part of this picture of newfound prosperity is the development in the area around Zamoranos of the iron-mining industry, with the first mine in operation by 1867 and a rapid growth in activity from the early years of the twentieth century.[144]

By 1908, there were fifteen textile mills in Priego, with a total of 278 legally registered looms (in comparison with just sixty-six in 1895). Since the sixteenth century, numerous mills had been

---

[142] Forcada Serrano, 2016, 38–39.

[143] Ibid., 49.

[144] Forcada Serrano, 2018, 163–69.

installed along the river as it descended from its source marked by the Fuente de la Salud to the level of the river Salado below the town. Now this hydraulic power could be transformed into electric energy, and this was done with spectacular success in the case of the industrial complex created in the gorge of Las Angosturas. Here, a factory using hand looms was established by José Ramón Matilla in 1902, and the construction of a dam and the installation of a turbine permitted the production of enough electricity to power a mill with almost fifty looms, leading to the creation of a village accommodating some 300 people. Other businesses in Priego, including both textile and olive oil mills, were quick to adopt the use of electricity, and both electric lighting and the more general use of electric power had both been introduced in the urban area by 1905. By the early 1920s, electric lighting was available in villages such as Zamoranos, Castil de Campos and El Cañuelo, although some others would have to wait up to a further half-century for it to be installed.[145]

Cotton mills sprang up in various parts of the town, including, for example, three in the heart of the old town in the area of the Adarve. The largest of these was established by Jerónimo Molina Sánchez in an imposing building that was adapted to house electric looms. Thirty-five of these were purchased from a Barcelona company in 1910 and, in due course, the number in operation rose to forty-two. Molina's factory supplied customers throughout Andalucía, Extremadura and central Spain.[146] For some time, the largest of the factories would be that of Rafael Molina Sánchez, situated in the appropriately named Calle Molinos. It already possessed thirty-seven looms in 1908 and by 1922 there were seventy-four. In 1907, the total number of looms recorded as functioning in Priego was 131. By the following year, it had risen to 278; and by 1915, it stood at 392.[147] In spite of its relative inaccessibility by

---

[145] Alcalá Ortiz, 2008, charts the early part of this process.
[146] Forcada Serrano, 2016, 54.
[147] Ibid., 58–59.

road and the absence of a railway to meet its obvious needs, Priego was developing into an industrial centre of undeniable importance. The contribution to the town's economy of the area's olive mills was also increasing steadily. By 1925, there were as many as 119 mills with a total of 169 presses, producing an annual total of 5,750,000 kg of olive oil. Nor should we forget the smaller but nonetheless valuable part played in the local economy by the 'San Luis' factory, which employed between 150 and 200 workers producing hats and was probably the single biggest employer in the area. It is not surprising that this period of dynamic growth in employment saw Priego's population rise from some 11,000 in 1857 to almost 17,000 in 1900 and 24,500 (greater, indeed, than its present-day population) in 1930.[148]

Las Angosturas
A general view of the groundbreaking industrial complex which was created in the gorge in the early years of the twentieth century. The construction of a dam and the installation of a turbine made it possible to generate sufficient electricity to power a mill with almost fifty looms. The village that grew up near the mill housed some 300 people. *Authorship of the photograph unknown.*

---

[148] Ibid., 66–67.

The town's economic difficulties had largely prevented any noteworthy progress in terms of its infrastructure during the first half of the nineteenth century. However, from about 1860, new projects became much more common, leading up to periods of 'building fever' such as that of the early 1890s.[149] Important developments included the new cemetery of San Luis (1859–65) and the initial work done on the ornamental gardens of the Paseo de Colombia (1874, but eventually acquiring its present form in 1898). A food market was constructed on the site of the old cloister of San Pedro, and new council buildings (though not the present one, which dates from the 1950s) were established where the Clarist convent had once stood. In the surrounding area, notably in the Calle Río, the prosperous middle classes built their impressive mansions and older houses were restored and extended.[150] Improvements were made to several streets and squares, and in the old walled quarter, where gateways, towers and battlements had long since been demolished, the Paseo del Adarve was remodelled. The early years of the twentieth century saw steady improvement to the town's infrastructure in terms of electricity and street lighting, mains water and drainage, urban transport and (from 1915) the telephone. The telegraph had already been installed in 1892.

However, the largest single new undertaking was the construction of the bullring on the site of an old stone quarry towards the western edge of the town. The project was launched in 1884 and the money was raised by private subscription, with a founding society of thirty-one members. The new *plaza* was finally officially opened on the 7th of August 1892.[151] Crucial for the town's economic and social progress was the opening up of new roads and transport services (by stage coach) to Cabra,

---

[149] Vera Aranda, 149.

[150] An interesting example is Calle Río, n° 33, built in the nineteenth century and restored at the beginning of the twentieth century. The birthplace of Niceto Alcalá-Zamora, it now houses a museum dedicated to his life and achievements.

[151] For a detailed account of the events leading up to the construction of Priego's bullring, see Forcada Serrano, 1992, 33–47.

Alcalá la Real and Granada. Equally significant, moreover, was the building of new roads to improve access to several of Priego's villages, advances which were associated above all with the appointment in 1917 of Niceto Alcalá-Zamora as the Government's Ministro de Fomento (Minister for Development).[152]

La Plaza del Palenque in about 1880, showing the theatre and (on the right) the Pósito or grain store, which had been built in the sixteenth century and was demolished in the 1930s. *Photograph by José García Ayola.*

This was also a period of noteworthy developments in Priego's cultural life. In 1915, the poet (and ex-mayor) Carlos Valverde López launched the local weekly newspaper *Patria Chica* ('Home Town'), containing a mixture of social commentary and cultural items. It declared itself to be politically neutral and without partisan bias, although its emphasis was unmistakeably socially conservative. It appeared every ten days and was a vigorous expression of local cultural achievement, but it lasted only seven months (from February to September), undoubtedly handicapped by hostility from the currently

---

[152] Alcalá Ortiz, 2002, 85–88.

dominant *'nicetista'* liberal faction. *Patria Chica* was representative of the burgeoning intellectual interests which characterised the Priego of its time and which were evident in the broad range of achievements of figures such as Carlos Valverde and Niceto Alcalá-Zamora. There were, of course, other outstanding individuals who made a distinctive contribution to that cultural life, and among these Francisco Ruiz Santaella and Adolfo Lozano Sidro, both born in Priego, deserve special mention. Ruiz Santaella had a variety of artistic interests, so broad that he has been dubbed 'Priego's Leonardo da Vinci', but he is best known as an architect, the inspiration behind several of the town's most impressive mansions. Lozano Sidro, although established as a highly successful artist in Madrid, where he became particularly well known as an illustrator of journals, magazines and books, returned regularly to his home town. His works include some memorable images of both high society and rural life.[153]

IV: Progress and prosperity – but not for all

In many respects, then, the early decades of the twentieth century were indeed a period of great economic and social advances for Priego. Carlos Valverde López, writing in *Patria Chica* in 1915, creates an idealised picture of a town which remained mercifully free from the shortages which were to be found in other parts of Spain:

> Without the support of large-scale capital investment or direction by great technical expertise, Priego has managed in certain branches of industry to achieve a highly favourable position among the towns and capital cities of the Peninsula. It owes all that it is to the effort and hard work of its offspring, to their boldness of character and to

---

[153] For Ruiz Santaella, see Alcalá Ortiz, 2008, 415, and for Lozano Sidro, the article by Herbert González Zymla in the *Diccionario Biográfico Español*.

the indomitable will-power which has always accompanied them, to the point of establishing our town as a first-class industrial centre. Hence the fact that the economic crises, dreadful in some other regions, driving the hungry classes to struggle to obtain the bread of which they are deprived, are unknown among us. The town's factories and workshops provide work for numerous people of both sexes, with the consoling guarantee that in the worker's home there will be no shortage of necessities and there will be no place for the distressing uncertainties by which predominantly agricultural communities are constantly beset.[154]

The house of José Serrano Ramos in the Calle Río
This was one of the characteristically modernist creations of the Priego architect Francisco Ruiz Santaella (1875–1950). *Photograph by Antonio Jesús Villena.*

---

[154] Quoted by Forcada Serrano, 2016, 61.

The Hidden Gem of the Subbética

En la Feria de Priego by Adolfo Lozano Sidro

Lozano Sidro (1872–1935) was born in Priego and, although he spent an important part of his career in Madrid, throughout his life he remained in close contact with his home town. His wide-ranging works include scenes of popular life, including this evocative image of the town's annual fair. Permission to hold the *feria* had first been granted in 1842 by Isabel II. It was both a market and a celebration, a time when country people and livestock dealers flocked to the town. The picture is displayed, together with a large collection of the artist's other work, in the museum situated in Calle Carrera de las Monjas. *The author is grateful to the Patronato Lozano Isidro for their permission to use this image.*

Cover illustration of the journal *Patria Chica*, September 1915

Published for the first time in February 1915, *Patria Chica* appeared three times each month. It was founded by the lawyer, writer and poet Carlos Valverde López. It claimed to be politically neutral, but it undoubtedly suffered as a result of hostility from the dominant liberal faction. It lasted for only seven months, and the edition that appeared on 1st September was the last but one. The illustration is by Adolfo Lozano Sidro, and the countrymen that they represent have the same dark-skinned, almost African look as those who figure in his painting of the *feria*. In the top left is the coat of arms of the town of Priego. *The author is grateful to the Biblioteca Nacional de España for permission to use this image.*

Immensely proud of his town and of what it had achieved, however, it seems that Valverde was inclined to exaggerate the extent to which Priego had escaped the difficulties of the time. He was right in the sense that it saw none of the explosive violence which resulted from the social tensions elsewhere, most notably in Catalonia, and that it avoided the growth of anarchism whose impact was most conspicuous in impoverished areas of rural Andalucía, where day labourers (*jornaleros*) eked out a living on the vast estates known as *latifundios*. However, there is undeniable evidence that in the Priego area there existed continuing hardship, immense social inequality and resulting friction.[155] Indeed, the very year in which Valverde wrote with such optimism saw one of 'the most tragic crises [of hunger] in terms both of the number of people affected and of the time that it lasted', and in an edition of *Patria Chica* published just three months after his article, we read of the despair of *jornaleros* who, 'on the wretched pittance that they earned could do no more than show bread to their children'.[156]

Moreover, if the rural workers' protests were not heard, it was precisely because they were in no position to express them. In these conditions, the workers of Priego, in view of their total dependence on the system of day labouring and, therefore, on the *señoritos*, unlike the workers in the towns of the *campiña* – such as Montilla, Espejo, Castro del Río – were unable to create their own class organisations and so gradually free themselves from the ideological domination of the oligarchy.[157]

---

[155] For a telling analysis of the huge contrast in living conditions between the privileged classes and the rural poor, see López Calvo, 65–76. Alcalá Ortiz, 2001, 69, points out that by 1923, 15% of the *término municipal* of Priego still belonged to the duque de Medinaceli, while much of the remainder was the property of a small number of landowners who exploited their land in ways which were (both technically and economically) archaic.

[156] Op. cit., 75.

[157] Op. cit., 74–75. A *señorito* is a term applied to a young person of means, but it was often (and continues to be) more generally used in an essentially pejorative sense to describe individuals who are wealthy and influential. For the *campiña cordobesa*, see note 138.

On the other hand, in Priego itself and in a number of its villages, workers' organisations did begin to take root during the first two decades of the twentieth century. In 1903, there was a strike in the San Luis hat factory which received support from workers' organisations in Barcelona but which was resolved through the mediation of Carlos Valverde López. Although Priego then remained free from industrial disputes for well over a decade, in 1916 there was a 'peaceful strike' and, significantly, on this occasion, among their other aims the workers sought an amnesty for political prisoners. Two years later, events in Priego reflected the unrest throughout the country when for a number of days the protests of various groups of workers coalesced into a general strike which paralysed the town's commercial and industrial activity. Support came from the villages, too, and the most conspicuous and militant example of this was from Zamoranos. The reasons for the strike were eloquently expressed in a pamphlet produced by workers' organisations in the villages of Fuente-Tójar, Zamoranos, Esparragal, El Cañuelo and Castil de Campos:

> The continuous increase in the cost of subsistence and the exaggerated cost of living in general, coupled with the shortage of work, has obliged workers throughout Spain to come together to request improvements with regard to the needs imposed by life in today's world.
>
> Almost everywhere they have won victories, if 'victory' is an appropriate word for attaining what can justly be requested and what is granted as such. However, in this area, which is more backward than anywhere else in the Peninsula and where the workers are less zealous in pursuing their own interests – doubtless on account of being less well informed – until now they have asked for nothing and so they have been given nothing. This is because the employers, busily involved in seeking out new markets for their products in order to increase their profits, have not bothered about the worker and would not bother about him unless they were forced to think about the matter.[158]

---

[158] For the full text of this pamphlet, see Cuadros Callava, 1998, 43.

It is a telling detail that in order not to give the impression of being subversive, the workers in their demonstration carried with them the Holy Sacrament. The factory owners agreed to increase wages, which were generally accepted as having been the lowest among textile workers throughout Spain. The bourgeoisie, however, were determined to put an end to the formation of independent workers' organisations and established a Workers' Centre for the Sons of Priego (Centro Obrero de Hijos de Priego), with the avowed aims of providing education and medical assistance and ensuring cooperation. The employers assumed control and the workers played only a passive part. The organisation was to achieve little and gradually peter out, with the workers once again retreating into their customary attitude of resignation.[159]

There were other reactions of various kinds to the desperate conditions which sometimes prevailed. In 1908, for example, a group of at least thirty families left Priego for Málaga, from where they set sail for South America. And, naturally enough, some individuals turned to crime. There are numerous cases of arrests for theft (of firewood, acorns, olives, poultry, etc.) and also of altercations and confrontations, sometimes with fatal consequences, all of this providing evidence of the tensions in society which resulted from deplorable living conditions. In a more extreme form, such tensions could lead to banditry, which well into the twentieth century remained common in areas quite close to Priego. One famous case is that of Antonio Mata Hidalgo, better known as Reverte, who at one stage in his lengthy criminal career headed a gang known as 'the Fuente-Tójar Three'.[160]

A particularly clear indicator of the level of social progress in the Priego area is the provision being made for education. This continued to be sorely deficient, and there can be no doubt that the level of illiteracy was very high. José Tomás Valverde, mayor

---

[159] López Calvo, op. cit., 81–85, gives a detailed and informative account of the events of the strike, its causes and its implications.

[160] Ibid., 125–34.

of Priego for six years in the 1920s, comments in his memoirs that while Priego should by rights have possessed twelve schools for boys, in fact it had only three, occupying rooms in private houses and lacking the most basic hygienic and pedagogical facilities.[161] Altogether, Priego possessed these three elementary schools for boys and two for girls, in addition to one for younger children. A total of 470 children were registered with them, but they had only the capacity to cope with 75% of that number. There was evidently a very high level of absenteeism, given that children were often required to work in the fields.[162] In those villages where schools did exist, the conditions were at least as basic as in the town: in Zamoranos, for example, it proved impossible to teach the thirty-five children registered with the school in the 16 square metres of space that were available.[163] There was no secondary school in Priego until the establishment of the Instituto Nacional de Segunda Enseñanza Alcalá-Zamora under the Second Republic in the 1930s. Many children received no formal education at all.

*

A series of weak Spanish governments proved unable to cope with the political and social tensions that continued to threaten the peace of the country, until in September 1923 General Miguel Primo de Rivera staged a virtually bloodless military coup and was accepted by King Alfonso XIII as Head of Government. He promised to restore order, create political stability and bring economic and social progress and, although under his control democratic freedoms were suppressed, his seizure of power was largely welcomed.

In Priego, under the dictatorship, a new council took control, led by José Tomás Valverde, a wealthy landowner who, like

---

[161] Valverde Castilla, 124.
[162] Del Caño Pozo, 29.
[163] Ruiz-Burruecos, 89.

Niceto Alcalá-Zamora, had trained as a lawyer. For the past decade, the allies of Alcalá-Zamora had exercised almost total dominance over political affairs in the town, but now they found themselves expelled from positions of power, and their administration was accused of having committed a range of irregularities. The division between the two factions, the *nicetistas* and the *valverdistas*, had first come to the fore in 1915 in the form of a dispute over Valverde's scheme for the installation of a network for drainage and the distribution of drinkable water, set out in an article in *Patria Chica*. It now became apparent in the implacable hostility that broke out in all manner of political, social and even religious contexts.[164] The new administration was savage in its condemnation of abuses committed under the authority of the *nicetistas*, and a particularly prominent part was played by Primo de Rivera's right-hand man, José Cruz Conde, who launched a bitter campaign aimed at discrediting Alcalá-Zamora.

In practice, the system of local government, characterised by abuse, patronage and victimisation, changed little under the dictatorship. Claims of injustice and law suits were common when land owned by Alcalá-Zamora and his supporters in what is now Calle Ramón y Cajal was expropriated for the construction of social housing.[165] There were extensive plans for the modernisation of infrastructure, but sometimes these were paralysed by lack of resources. For example, what was then Calle Alcalá-Zamora and is now Calle Río was impassable for three years because of unfinished work on drainage and the installation of water piping.[166] The plan to exploit sources of

---

[164] The rivalry in religious matters took the form of the two families' attachment to different *cofradías*: the Alcalá-Zamoras were closely associated with the *Cofradía de la Columna*, while the Valverdes played a leading role in the *Hermandad del Nazareno*. For an examination of this and other aspects of the confrontations between *nicetistas* and *valverdistas*, see Alcalá Ortiz, 2001, 127–68.

[165] Cuadros Callava, 1988, 35.

[166] A century later, though in much less acrimonious times, Calle Río would again be closed to traffic for an extended period while similar work was being carried out.

water near the Fuente de la Salud ran into serious practical difficulties and led to the water supply to houses of the *nicetistas* being systematically cut off and to consequent demands to begin the work again. The financial implications were to prove a heavy burden.

Nevertheless, valuable and undeniable progress was made with respect to the quality of life for the people of Priego. Improvement of drainage and the provision of mains water, concluding the process of covering over the course of the river through the town, the construction of public wash-houses (helping to avoid the contamination of clean water), the paving of several streets and the opening of a much-needed access road (Calle Cava), the completion of Priego's first public park (Paseo de Colombia), the establishment of a municipal pharmacy, the refurbishment of the slaughterhouse and meat market, the creation of an interurban telephone system, the extension and improvement of public lighting in the town and its installation in some villages, and the opening of negotiations for the acquisition of a site for a new town hall: all of this amounted to a concerted and coherent programme which not only sought to improve radically the town's infrastructure but also created work opportunities and thus reduced emigration. New schools were created in Priego itself and in some villages (Campo Nubes and Lagunillas). The stability and sense of progress during Primo de Rivera's dictatorship and Valverde's administration was to be seen by many during the Civil War years and the difficult post-war period as a kind of golden age.[167]

Particularly in view of the area's important production of both

---

[167] Cuadros Callava, 1988, 37–45, gives a balanced account of both the difficulties and the progress made in Priego during the period of dictatorship. His conclusion with regard to José Tomás Valverde's contribution is similarly even-handed. He praises 'the honesty and economic transparency of his administration' and what Valverde achieved, for example, with regard to provision for health and social benefits, but he also criticises his prominent part in the political persecution of Alcalá-Zamora and his followers, 'which provoked serious confrontations and rivalries in the region and had harmful consequences that took years to disappear'.

textiles (in 1925, there were twenty-two mills with 612 looms) and olive oil (119 mills with 169 presses), it was crucial for Priego that the network of communications – by road and, if possible, by rail – should be improved. The total weight of produce that needed to be transported to and from the town each year was 16,006,000 kg.[168] In 1925, in response to the announcement of a new national plan for the extension of the railway network, a report was produced which set out clearly the poor state of the local roads and made the case for a rail link. It was obvious that Priego's very high transport costs put the town at a serious disadvantage commercially, but for a time there was real hope that the dreamed-for railway might be built, not only permitting further rapid industrial progress but even opening up opportunities for the town's impressive artistic heritage to attract tourists.

There were great hopes for the future, but they were soon to be dashed. This was in part through lack of enterprise and vision on the part of the town's employers, who failed to collaborate in order to make the most of the opportunities.[169] It was, however, the political, social and economic turmoil of the following years which was, in Priego as elsewhere in Spain, to put an end to such aspirations.

---

[168] Forcada Serrano, 2016, 63.
[169] Cuadros Callava, 1988, 39.

CHAPTER 7

The Tempestuous Decade

∽

I: From dictatorship to republic: the president's home town

The Spanish government's excessive spending had led to serious economic problems, and the end of Primo de Rivera's dictatorship came rapidly. It became increasingly apparent that he had lost the confidence of most of the influential groups in Spanish society, including his fellow army officers and the king himself. In January 1930, he resigned and left Spain; he died a few months later. This in itself did not mean the end of the monarchy. Alfonso XIII appointed another army officer, General Berenguer, in Primo de Rivera's place, and for over a year the new government survived in the form of what was known colloquially as the 'soft dictatorship' or *dictablanda*. Debilitated by indecision and undermined by growing support for republicanism, the government's control over events weakened dangerously. When municipal elections were held on 14th April 1931, although nationally the monarchists won most votes, the provincial capitals voted overwhelmingly for republican candidates. Alfonso XIII went into exile just two days later.

In Priego, a *nicetista* council had been returned to power in February 1930: in view of Alcalá-Zamora's national role (in August, he was appointed president of the Revolutionary Committee which was later to become the Provisional Government), it was said that here the Second Republic arrived a year ahead of the rest of Spain.[170] In the April 1931 municipal elections, the *valverdistas* emerged victorious with sixteen councillors to eight, probably as a result of José Tomás Valverde's previous achievements as mayor, but, with the declaration of the Republic in Madrid, this result was annulled. In protest, the *valverdistas* boycotted the re-election, which took place a month later.

By now, Priego was occupying a prominent position on the national stage, for immediately after the April election Niceto Alcalá-Zamora had been chosen to head the new government as Prime Minister, and in December 1931 he was elected first President of the Republic, a position which he was to hold until May 1936. His situation was not without difficulty, however, particularly given the evident clash between his devout Catholicism (as reflected in his involvement in Priego's Cofradía de la Columna) and the new government's hardline anti-clerical policies.

The tension in Priego that had marked the relationship between the town's two political factions quickly came to the fore: on the same day that the Republic was declared, a prominent *valverdista* was shot dead in a confrontation with the municipal police. Subsequent disputes, although they did not reach such extremes, were constant and bitter. In August 1932, José Tomás Valverde, together with two of his supporters, was accused of complicity in General Sanjurjo's failed coup and was imprisoned for two months.[171] In September, there occurred a bizarre and controversial episode when the President of the Republic visited his home town during the town's *feria*. A bullfight was organised for the afternoon, to be attended by Alcalá-Zamora, the Socialist minister Indalecio Prieto and the civil governor of Córdoba. Unexpectedly, it seems, to the acute embarrassment of the president, the *plaza* was almost empty. The

---

[170] Forcada Serrano, 1997, 193.

[171] General José Sanjurjo's rebellion against the Republic, in which he was supported by a number of Carlists and other army officers, was proclaimed in Sevilla, where it achieved initial success, but in Madrid it was a complete failure.

valverdistas argued that the people of the town had stayed away as a protest against the treatment of the ex-mayor, but the *nicetistas*, on the other hand, claimed that their opponents had bought up the tickets in order to leave the event without spectators. The truth of the matter has never been established, but there could be no more telling example of the nature of the futile disputes which dogged Priego in the pre-war years.[172]

Nevertheless, valuable contributions were made during the years of the Republic to social welfare in Priego and the surrounding area.[173] Work continued on the paving of streets and the provision of mains water and drainage, along with improvements to public fountains. The food market, established in 1905 on lands belonging to the convent of San Pedro (and which had previously been operated as a private enterprise), was now renovated and given a new roof. The old prison was demolished and a new one was built on the site of the present-day bus station.

Important advances were made in education, in which up to this point the lack of resources had kept the town 'at a medieval level'.[174] A School of Arts and Trades (Escuela de Artes y Oficios) was opened to provide the basis of a professional training and – a particularly significant development – a secondary school was opened in a house situated in what under the Republic was renamed Calle Alcalá-Zamora (but is now once again known as the Calle Río). A site was acquired for the construction of a larger and more appropriate building, although this decision was to be rapidly reversed after the Nationalist uprising in 1936. The Pósito (the grain store, an elegant edifice which had stood since the sixteenth century in the square of El Palenque – see Chapter 4) was demolished and a school for young girls constructed on

---

[172] Forcada Serrano, 1992, 63–67, examines the evidence for both accounts of the events.

[173] Alcalá Ortiz, 2002, 69–128, provides an extensive survey of what was achieved for Priego and its villages during Niceto Alcalá-Zamora's time as President of the Republic.

[174] Ibid., 96.

the site, and a school for boys was built in the Calle San Luis behind the hat factory.[175] A library was installed in the secondary school. Highly indicative, too, of the Republic's programme to bring education as broadly as possible to the working people were the plans to establish a network of twenty-three schools in the villages around Priego, involving the construction of thirty-nine houses for teachers.

In other respects, too, attempts were made to introduce basic improvements in order to raise the quality of life in the villages, notably (given that some of them would still have to wait almost half a century for mains water) the construction of fountains and wash-houses. Several such facilities were provided at the president's own expense, for example, the one built to serve El Poleo and Las Higueras, opened in 1934 but reconstructed some four years later after being damaged, presumably by shellfire, during the Civil War.

The provision of such facilities was by no means Niceto Alcalá-Zamora's only personal contribution to the financing of public works. Another example was the construction of seven houses in the Calle San Marcos, which were offered rent-free to needy families. Although they were of poor quality, they were occupied for several years until eventually the houses and the building plot were given by Alcalá-Zamora's daughters – after his death and the family's return from exile – to the Church. The present church of La Trinidad was built on the site.

Alcalá-Zamora's term as president did not last until the end of the Republic. He was dismissed by the *Cortes* in April 1936. Detested by the right as the epitome of republican values and out of sympathy with what he saw as the excesses of the left,

---

[175] The demolition of the Pósito (which had been acquired by the Council in 1908 and which the Valverde administration had planned to convert into a town hall) is generally considered to have been the most serious mistake made in Priego under the Republic in terms of urban development. Vera Aranda, 151, suggests that the destruction of this and a number of other public buildings dating from the sixteenth century was intended to demonstrate a sharp break with the past.

he ended his days a lonely figure living in relative poverty in Buenos Aires. The mockery that his political opponents in Priego directed at him is evident in a popular song of the 1930s:

Un martes de primavera	One Tuesday in Spring,
echaste de España al Rey.	you threw out Spain's king.
Y otro martes de abril era	Another Tuesday in April
cuando te echó España entera	the whole of Spain in turn
por conducto de la ley.	threw you out – by right.
Como un cohete subió	Like a rocket he shot up
hacia la altura infinita	to the infinite heights,
en la altura reventó	but up there he burst apart
y del cohete quedó	and nothing more was left
sólo el carrizo y la guita.	than the stick – and the cash.
– Pura, me voy de viaje	– Pura, I'm going away,
hacia países remotos.	off to distant lands.
– ¿Y qué llevas de equipaje?	– What are you taking?
– Pues este traje que traje,	– Just this suit I brought,
dos botas y cinco votos.	two boots – and five votes.[176]

'Pura', who is addressed here, is María de la Purificación Castillo Bidaburu, the president's wife. The mention of 'botas' is an allusion to the nickname given to Alcalá-Zamora by his opponents on account of the shining elasticated boots that he often wore. After the war, Priego, which undoubtedly suffered discrimination because of its connection with him, was to be disparagingly known by the regime as 'el pueblo (the town) de Las Botas'.

---

[176] Alcalá Ortiz, 1992, 323–24.

This **statue of Niceto Alcalá-Zamora,** the work of Priego artist Antonio Serrano, was erected on the Plaza de la Constitución (in front of the town hall) in December 2021 to mark the 90th anniversary of Alcalá-Zamora's installation as President of Spain's Second Republic. In 2023, it was moved to a location outside his birthplace in the newly restored Calle Río. *Photograph by Félix Javier Serrano Serrano.*

A much more balanced assessment of Alcalá-Zamora's qualities and faults is given by Hugh Thomas in his history of the Civil War:

> The first Prime Minister of the republic was Niceto Alcalá-Zamora, a barrister from Andalusia, with the flowery style of eloquence typical of that region. Warm-hearted, honest, erudite and confident, Alcalá-Zamora was also vain and meddlesome, and, while in Madrid he appeared to love liberty more than life, he seemed the embodiment of the old-time political boss in Priego, his remote home town in the south.[177]

---

[177] Thomas, 33.

II: July 1936 – April 1939. Priego during the Civil War

By the summer of 1936, the Madrid government had largely lost control of events. In different parts of Spain, estates were being seized by rural workers hoping to turn into reality the promised redistribution of land, and in cities there was a spiral of street violence. Political forces had become polarised: the Falange Española, of fascist ideology, was growing in strength, and various right-wing groups (notably important elements of the armed forces) were conspiring to rebel against the Republican government. Viewing themselves as a national movement, they came to be known as *nacionales* (Nationalists). On 13th July, the charismatic right-wing civilian leader José Calvo Sotelo was assassinated by Assault Guards in a revenge killing, and this proved to be the crucial event which sparked the rebellion. The uprising began on 17th July in Morocco and on the following day it spread to the Peninsula. In parts of Spain (notably the predominantly rural areas of northern Spain and in some major cities such as Sevilla), there was little resistance. Other regions, however (and most significantly Madrid and Barcelona), remained loyal to the Republic. In September, General Francisco Franco became not only Supreme Commander of the Nationalist forces but also Head of State, a position which he was to continue to occupy until his death in 1975. Spain found itself split into two zones, and the remainder of the war was to see the slow but inexorable advance of the Nationalists into Republican territory. The process was notoriously brutal and unforgiving.

In Priego, a small group of members of the Falange had been in existence since the foundation of the organisation in 1933 and on the morning of 18th July, the local Falangist leader was quick to offer the lieutenant of the *Guardia Civil* the support of 200 men.[178] A command post was set up in a private house in the

---

[178] Cuadros Callava, 2019, 54. This informative study has been an invaluable source of information on events in Priego during the war, and much of the account which follows is based on it.

centre of Priego and panic rapidly spread among the Falange's political opponents, not least when news came through of the successful uprising in Sevilla headed by General Queipo de Llano. The *nicetistas*, taking false encouragement from the fact that the general was Alcalá-Zamora's son-in-law, opted to offer no resistance, and the Falangists were soon in complete control of the streets. Potential opponents appear to have surrendered meekly, not understanding the significance of events. By the next day, the first dead body was in evidence, strings of prisoners were being led into confinement and preparations were being made for the defence of the town against attack. In the next few days, some of the town's leading socialist politicians were arrested and shot. A column of Falangists moved on the village of Castil de Campos and detained militant socialist leaders, initially with a view to executing them immediately. A period of unprecedented violence and repression was about to begin.

On 22nd July, José Tomás Valverde arrived in Priego. Since May 1935, he had been vice-president of Renovación Española, an organisation closely linked to the Falange. Essentially, his task was to oversee a total political reorganisation of the town. Francisco Adame, the Republican mayor, pledged his support for the uprising and continued in office until, a fortnight later, on the 4th of August, the existing town council was disbanded and replaced by a body entirely sympathetic to the objectives and ideals of the Nationalists. Moreover, a new military commander, Lieutenant Roldán Écija, was installed, and he rapidly set about the elimination of what he termed the 'Marxist poison'. Armed units made up of Nationalist supporters in Priego were dispatched to the surrounding villages to consolidate the authority of the Nationalists throughout the area.

In the country as a whole, the policy of the new regime was to impose total control through brutality and terror, and what Priego experienced was no exception to this. The study by Cuadros Callava sets out clearly what it meant in practice, illustrating how the army, the Civil Guard and the Falange, backed up by the clergy and a network of informants, combined to root out dissident elements and to impose an absolute orthodoxy through a process which went beyond imprisonment, torture and execution and included psychological humiliation, economic exploitation and the total ruin of families:

> Not only did this combination spread fear and dread among the population but it also served to control behaviour, morality and even the way of thinking of the vast majority of Priego's society, made up essentially of small business owners, textile workers and day labourers ... The repression and the subsequent reprisals which took place in Priego, without any cause or justification, achieved their aims. Their double effect – to terrify liberal-progressive society and to bind together the valverdista-conservative element – established it as one of the pillars which supported the Francoist regime over the following decades.[179]

It appears probable that, between the outbreak of the conflict and the post-war period, the number of those who were killed or disappeared from Priego and the villages is about 200, far greater than the officially recorded figure (of no more than twenty), and there is evidence of the existence of mass graves, two of them within Priego's municipal cemetery.[180] Victims were both male and female and, in addition, many women who were accused of pro-Republican sympathies were subject to grotesque acts of public humiliation.[181]

The process of repression, of course, went further. It included the confiscation of the property and other resources of those considered to be enemies of the regime or whose conduct was seen as inappropriate in any of numerous ways. In rural areas, property, livestock and crops were freely plundered (by troops of both sides, given Priego's proximity

---

[179] Cuadros Callava, 2019, 73.

[180] Ibid., 85–86.

[181] See, for example, the personal testimonies recorded by Ignacio Muñiz, 2009, 71–73.

to the front). Public employees had to demonstrate beyond doubt their loyalty to and support for the Nationalists' ideals and values. A number of teachers in Priego's primary schools were removed from their posts, following a process of investigation which began within a week of the Nationalist uprising, and books not considered appropriately moral or patriotic were banned.[182] In an act of particular vindictiveness, the town's only secondary school, which bore the name of Niceto Alcalá-Zamora, was closed, thus depriving generations of Priego's children of the right to pursue secondary studies in their own town. Severe measures were enforced against all allies of Niceto Alcalá-Zamora, and reprisals against his family, friends and supporters were to continue until well after the war. Not surprisingly, by September 1936, the authorities had already changed numerous street names: so, for example, the streets previously known as 'Alcalá-Zamora' and 'Prim' (after the liberal revolutionary of the 1860s) now acquired the names of 'Héroes de Toledo' (commemorating the defenders of the Nationalist stronghold in Toledo's *alcázar*) and 'José Antonio Primo de Rivera' (after the founder of the Falange).[183]

Of course, not all that happened was systematic or planned, and the people of the countryside grew accustomed to the fear of living close to the front. Enrique Cabello Povedano describes his experience of living in La Carrasca as a child:

> The 'reds' were on the other side of the river, you know? The river runs down below us, doesn't it? That area was in the hands of the 'reds' and it was the river that marked the front. That is why, when they came over, we had to run up to escape ... I can't remember now, but one of them got into a hayloft that was for animals, and he was killed. In the war a lot of people were killed. They killed my father ... my father. They said that he must have died on the front, but in fact he was with the soldiers in El Poleo.

---

[182] For details of the measures taken against teachers and schools, see Del Caño Pozo, 65–103.

[183] These are now Calle Río and Calle Carrera de las Monjas respectively.

In those days I was living in La Carrasca and I was just two years old, something like that. People used to go out hunting ... nowadays you have to have a licence ... and he was with the soldiers. 'Let's give him a bit of a fright,' they said. And a bullet went straight through him.[184]

The new school building constructed in the Palenque in the 1930s, after the demolition of the Pósito

Teaching began in the new school (initially known as 'Escultor Álvarez') in 1935, but after the military uprising in the following year it was renamed 'Emilio Fernández' after a young member of the right-wing Falange movement who died on the front. It was eventually transferred – on account of its bad state of repair and lack of facilities – to the Casa de Cultura in Calle Río. This photograph emphasises the yoke and arrows, the symbol of Franco's regime. *Details of the photographer unknown.*

---

[184] From an interview recorded with the author.

Priego, which for such a long period of its history had been a frontier town, now found itself very close to the front between the Nationalist and Republican zones. The river Caicena, flowing north-westwards from Almedinilla, marked the actual front line of the conflict, and the trenches and emplacements still clearly visible on the Cerro de las Cabezas near Fuente-Tojar represent one of the most advanced points occupied by the Nationalist forces. Following the failure of the Republican army's attack on Córdoba in August 1936, the line between the opposing forces on this part of the front remained essentially unchanged for most of the war, with Priego serving as a divisional command centre under Lieutenant Colonel Rafael de las Morenas. In fact, the only incident resulting directly from military action which affected the town was the dropping of a number of bombs in October 1937, leading to a small number of deaths in the area of the castle and in the Carrera del Águila.

In some respects, the working life of the town of Priego carried on through the war years with a surprising degree of normality. At least twenty cotton mills continued to function, giving employment to almost 600 people. In spite of a shortage of raw materials and an irregular electricity supply, well over a million and a half metres of cloth were produced in a year. There was no forgetting the political backdrop, however. For the textile companies, as in other social and economic contexts, the prominent display of the slogans of Franco's regime in any communication was rigorously enforced.[185]

It is frequently argued that in comparison with most towns and cities in Andalucía, Priego escaped many of the horrors of the war. It is true that it did not see the mass executions, imprisonments and reprisals that took place elsewhere. There had been a very limited presence of supporters of radical left-wing or revolutionary ideologies before the war broke out, and the town had come under Nationalist control from the very

---

[185] Forcada Serrano, 2016, 76–77.

first day of the uprising. Many will argue that it saw relatively little in terms of direct conflict and that in this it was fortunate indeed. Others will point out that in both Priego itself and in its villages the brutal process of repression and victimisation left a long-lasting scar on 'a population covered by a dark blanket of silence imposed by an elite which acted against democratic legality'.[186]

---

[186] Cuadros Callava, 2019, 238.

CHAPTER 8

Colossus with Feet of Clay

∞

I: Growth

Nominally, Spain's civil war ended on 1st April 1939, but in reality the consequences of the conflict would continue to be felt long afterwards. Not only was there no end to the persecution of those deemed to be the regime's enemies but, in addition, anti-Francoist resistance still operated in areas not far from Priego, notably in the mountains of the Sierra Sur of Jaén. Today, the older residents of some of Priego's villages still talk of the exploits of the guerrilla group led by Tomás Villén Roldán, known as 'Cencerro' ('the Cowbell'), which carried out a successful and provocative campaign against the Civil Guard until the death of its leader in 1947. In 1946, a shoot-out in Fuente-Tójar led to at least six deaths, and in 1950, a major operation by the Civil Guard wiped out guerrilla groups still operating in the Priego area.[187]

Spain had entered a long period of political repression and economic difficulty. The wartime nature of the regime was evident and more generally its policies favoured those sections of society that had supported the 1936 rebellion. Social and economic measures reflected a fascist ideology, with an emphasis on the nation's self-sufficiency, on high tariff barriers, on state intervention in business and on government control of

---

[187] Cuadros Callava, 2019, 229–30. There is a lively and very readable account of the struggle between the Civil Guard and the resistance fighters in Almudena Grandes' novel *El lector de Julio Verne* (*The Reader of Jules Verne*).

industry. The role of the Church was fundamental in lending its total support to the regime and providing it with what it considered to be its essentially Christian ideology; only in the 1970s did the Spanish Church adopt a much more radically independent stance.

Priego had lost all the importance at a national level that it had acquired through its association with Niceto Alcalá-Zamora. Indeed, its connection with the ex-president of the Republic now counted heavily against it in the government's thinking. A particularly vindictive act which reflected this attitude was the closure of the town's secondary school in 1937 (see Chapter 7). It was sixteen years before any secondary qualifications could be obtained in any of Priego's schools (in what was eventually to become the Instituto Fernando III el Santo), and even then the school was open just to boys. Only from the end of the 1960s were girls able to undertake secondary studies in Priego.

Paradoxically, however, while the post-war years saw relatively little progress in Priego in terms of infrastructure and urban development, and while, for many, this was a time of hardship and often hunger, the town's textile industry flourished to an unprecedented degree.[188]

By 1943, there were thirty-two cotton mills in Priego and (according to an official survey) a total of 663 looms. These numbers had actually doubled since before the Civil War. According to figures published the previous year in a Falangist journal, an average of 90,000 metres of fabric were being produced every week, with employment being provided for over a thousand workers. The cloth was being sold in Andalucía, Extremadura, central Spain and Levante (the area around Valencia). New factories were opening and new owners were

---

[188] Forcada Serrano, 1997, 197. Forcada points to a double paradox: the earlier part of the Francoist era brought an industrial boom but little social and cultural development, while the later years (the 1960s and 1970s) were characterised by industrial decline but by much more positive progress with regard to the evolution of the town and its infrastructure and services.

entering the market. In addition, there was rapid growth in the number of small semi-official enterprises, many of them family-based, which produced articles of clothing or household items; these items were not always of high quality but the businesses did provide an important income that offered an escape from poverty. This growth in small companies, in many cases destined not to last for more than just a few years, was favoured by the Francoist government's commitment – given Spain's position in the 1940s of political and economic isolation – to a policy of national self-reliance, and in 1946, legislation gave specific encouragement to home-based textile workers.[189]

On the other hand, in contrast with this picture of prosperity, it is important not to forget the plight of the not inconsiderable number of employers who fell victim of the political reprisals characteristic of the years following the war. This was the case, for instance, with Pedro Morales Serrano, a factory owner who suffered economic sanctions (including exile from Priego) as a result of his friendship with Niceto Alcalá-Zamora.[190]

There were practical problems which affected the industry, too, principally the cost of electricity and the shortage of raw materials, and the situation was aggravated by a number of other factors including the effects of the black market and an environment which favoured those well connected with the regime. Especially harmful for Priego was the national quota system by which the quantity of raw material allocated to an area was proportionate to the capacity that it already possessed, and in this respect Priego and other Andalusian industrial centres could not compete with Cataluña. In addition, as the weavers were dependent on the supply of cotton thread – of which the Catalan producers had a virtual monopoly – in practice, the Priego looms received far less than their due of their basic raw material. The same applied to supplies of chemicals and other essential products.

---

[189] For a detailed analysis of these developments in the post-war years, see Forcada Serrano, 2016, 77–83.

[190] See Cuadros Callava, 2015, 4.

Undeniably, the post-war years saw many cases of extreme hardship, with salaries, even in the textile industry, unable to meet the requirements of a reasonable standard of living. Numerous families received assistance from charitable organisations: the Conferencia de San Vicente collected money and distributed it to the most needy on a weekly basis; Acción Católica likewise provided help in extreme cases, and some private individuals made substantial contributions. The *cofradías* and *hermandades* also provided assistance, including through the provision of meals and notably on the occasion of religious festivals.[191]

Nevertheless, ten years after the end of the Civil War, Priego remained a flourishing centre for the textile industry and possessed a total of thirty-two factories, in comparison, for example, with the thirteen that existed in the city of Granada. In the subsequent decade, the situation was to improve still further. Nationally, foreign trade increased considerably and, while on the one hand this allowed easier access to raw materials – in this case cotton – on the other it gave an enormous boost to exports, especially of olive oil. New olive mills were constructed, the production process was improved and the Cooperative 'La Purísima' was established in 1945. In consequence, the spending power of the community, both urban and rural, increased, providing a further incentive for the expansion of the textile industry. Government policy gave further encouragement through the promotion of the cultivation of cotton in the Guadalquivir valley and the establishment of large-scale cotton ginning companies such as HYTASA (based in Seville but among whose founders was José Carrillo Montoro, a native of Priego) and CEPANSA, which in the 1950s established factories for spinning and weaving cotton in Mérida, Córdoba and Priego de Córdoba.[192] From 1950, the industry's raw material could be

---

[191] Forcada Serrano, 2017, 90.

[192] 'Ginning' is the process by which cotton is separated from seeds and other debris. The deseeded and cleaned cotton is then baled and sold to a mill for further processing.

obtained directly from these companies, and its dependence on Catalan suppliers was at an end.

In 1948, negotiations between the (government-controlled) trade union and Priego's town council culminated in the decision to establish a training school/workshop for the textile industry, backed by a substantial budget. It came into existence at the beginning of the following year with the title of the 'Taller-Escuela Sindical de Formación Profesional Textil Virgen del Buen Suceso' with the stated objective of meeting the varied training needs of forty-six textile companies with a total of over 1,200 registered workers. Its ambitions even included the re-establishment of the silk industry, from the planting of mulberry trees to the elaboration of the fabrics. Premises were rented in Calle Superunda and the school continued to function until 1970, with a number of students that varied between thirty in its initial year and fifty-nine in 1966–67.

The 1950s and the beginning of the 1960s saw Priego's textile industry at its height, and it was probably in 1963 that it reached its peak in terms of both the number of looms (well over 1,000) and its level of activity. The number of looms increased steadily over this period and several of the factories continued to modernise, making substantial investment, notably in automatic looms. In 1958, for instance, the factory at Las Angosturas produced a total of 267,326 metres of cloth. Particularly prominent, however, is the example of the company which in 1943 acquired the name of 'Textil del Carmen S.A.' and whose premises stood between Calle Cava and Calle Ramón y Cajal. It was in 1954 that this company made a huge investment in machinery purchased from a Barcelona company, enabling it to carry out all parts of the processing to a very high standard. It could now claim to employ sixty-seven people, including fifty women, and to have increased its annual production capacity to 440,000 metres of woven cloth. Textil del Carmen S.A., headed by the three Linares Montero brothers, José, Francisco and Antonio, remained for several years at the head of its sector in Priego and in 1967 it possessed 108 looms and had 126 employees. By the end of 1976, however, it would cease to exist, leaving a total of ninety workers redundant, including forty-nine women.[193]

The extent to which the success of the textile industry at its height fed into almost every aspect of Priego's social fabric is summarised in a report written in 1959:

> In recent years, Priego's textile industry has had a decisive effect on the town's economic prosperity, since the wages from over a thousand permanent jobs have been transformed into a commercial movement with an impact on a range of businesses highly diverse in character ... every week the leisure industry, food shops, clothing, silks and cottons, theatres and cinemas, etc., are enjoying the constant custom of textile workers. At the same time these commercial centres are extending this area of influence to a number of hamlets and villages in the surrounding district.[194]

Strikingly, the report went on to point out that the high number of females employed in the textile industry, who thus became the family's principal wage earner, was proving problematic in that the husband was being deprived of his traditional role as head of the family. On the other hand, the establishment and rapid growth of the Nuestra Señora del Carmen children's nursery was hailed as a notable step forward.

It was indeed not only in terms of industrial output that the 1950s and early 1960s could be looked back on as halcyon days in the development of modern Priego. The town's 'Casino' (or social and cultural association) had been founded in 1848 and had its premises in the Calle Carrera de las Monjas (in the post-war period known as Calle José Antonio). Under the presidency of José Luis Gamiz Valverde, it set about a process of modernisation, redefining its functions and extending its

---

[193] For an account of the achievements of Textil del Carmen S.A., see Forcada Serrano, 2017, 105–11.

[194] Matilla Rivadeneyra, 12.

activities. Gamiz Valverde played a vital and varied role as a sponsor and promoter of the arts. Under the Republic he had been first a teacher of Philosophy and then head teacher of the Instituto Niceto Alcalá-Zamora. Now, under his direction, the Casino's Section of Literature and Arts undertook an ambitious programme of cultural events including wide-ranging lectures and concerts, and at the end of August 1948 the first in a long and distinguished series of festivals of music and dance took place in the gardens of the 'Huerta de las Infantas', otherwise known as the 'Recreo de Castilla' (after the Castilla family, owners of the gardens).[195] From 1959, Priego was included among the select group of centres for the Ministry of Information and Tourism's national programme of festivals, and it proceeded to host a variety of cultural events including national and international drama, ballet and *zarzuelas*.[196] Even the provincial capital of Córdoba itself was not included in this prestigious group of venues.

It was also under the auspices of the Section of Literature and Arts that in October 1952 Priego's journal *Adarve* produced its first edition. Taking its name from the natural balcony that ran along the edge of the old town, *Adarve* initially appeared each week. The expression of the publication's dedication to the ideals of Franco's regime which opens that first issue reflects clearly the care and tact with which such an enterprise had to be approached, but it also goes on to set out *Adarve*'s aims and aspirations, reflecting a powerful sense of pride in Priego's past achievements and optimism for its future. This dedication is worth quoting in full for what it tells us of the spirit of its age:

> The appearance of this first number of ADARVE coincides with the date on which Spain commemorates how the Supreme General of the Armed Forces, Francisco Franco Bahamonde, first assumed the role of Head of the Spanish State. As members of the

---

[195] Manuel Mendoza Carreño, 40–55, describes these activities in detail.

[196] *Zarzuela* is a traditional Spanish genre of light opera, combining music and dialogue, often involving regional themes and settings.

national community, the producers of this weekly newspaper take pride in the General's leadership and our loyalty has no limits; and so, as the publication and the anniversary coincide, let its first lines be dedicated to him, with the desire that Heaven will grant his person all possible favour and that day by day beneath his command our Homeland will become greater and more prosperous.

GREETINGS: ADARVE sees the light of day amidst a sense of great anticipation, the enthusiasm of youth and hope rich with promise. Modest, simple, clean in conscience and at the same time full of the finest intentions. Its noble aspiration is for Priego to possess the well-deserved vehicle for communication which is necessary in modern times. This is a difficult and complex task which will undoubtedly not be without its thorny and awkward moments; an honourable undertaking, seeking no profit, specifically created in order to cultivate the eternal values of the spirit (which are essential to the appreciation of material matters); in short, a thoroughly worthwhile mission which the Section of Literature and Arts of Priego's Casino will oversee with enthusiasm. ADARVE extends its arms in brotherly greeting to all the people of Priego and to those who live with them, promising them reliable information and opinions which are calmly formed, objective and independent, at all times free from distorted or superficial interpretations. It will mark a step forward with regard to everything that represents progress, the protection of the municipal area, industrial activity or the encouragement of commerce. Its readers, both distinguished and humble, will always meet with warm support for their just demands. From its established viewing-points, a bastion of past glories, it will keep an ambitious watch over the prestige and grandeur of the Town. With an unbreakable faith in the supreme national destiny, ADARVE offers its warmest respects to Spain's leader, to her Government (in particular the Most Excellent Minister of Information and Tourism) and the provincial and local authorities. It sends affectionate and effusive greetings to its dear colleagues in Cabra at La Opinión and El Popular. ADARVE begins its altruistic undertaking without exaggerated use of platitudes or high-sounding expressions and concepts; confident in what it does, ambitious in its efforts and persevering in its sacrifices. It is with pleasure that it presents itself to the public and submits to the critics, because it knows in advance that definitive judgement on it will depend only on the test of time.

Adarve was edited by José Luis Gamiz Valverde, and its publication was uninterrupted until his death in 1968, by when 822 issues had appeared. It was revived in May 1976, with two editions being published each month, and it continues today to be an important feature of Priego's cultural life.

1952 saw the completion and inauguration of the new town hall, built on the central site once occupied by the Clarissan convent. It was, and remains, an impressive edifice, combining an attractive wedding-cake exterior with an imposing and spacious interior. In terms of new building, however, this represented an isolated highlight. In general, the principal features of Priego's development during the first decade and a half of the Francoist period have been defined as 'a lack of urban planning, only slight growth of the town (driven by increasing demographic pressure), a certain anarchy in the construction (although this was inconsequential in view of the small amount of growth) and a slowing down of public works'.[197] Perhaps surprisingly the situation was to see little improvement over the following two decades, with an aggressive approach to construction leading to the disfiguring of streets such as Calle Río, chaotic organisation in areas such as La Moraleda and the loss of important buildings such as the Baroque sanctuary of La Virgen de la Cabeza, which collapsed in the 1960s. The last of these events has been seen as symptomatic of the general decline which was to overtake the town in the years which followed.[198]

In spite of the serious deficiencies in urban planning, however, Priego undeniably underwent numerous positive changes which improved the quality of life for its citizens during this period of prosperity. 1953 saw the establishment of a

---

[197] Vera Aranda, 152.
[198] Forcada Serrano, 2000, 351.

secondary school, which was initially known as the Centro de Enseñanza Media y Profesional de Priego de Córdoba ('Priego de Córdoba Centre for Intermediate and Professional Education') and subsequently came to be known as the Instituto Fernando III el Santo, taking its name from the monarch who had first conquered madīnat Bāguh in the early thirteenth century. It was situated initially in Calle Río and by 1956 part of the building had been adapted for boarding. At first, places were for boys only and the courses offered were limited and essentially vocational. Not until the 1970s would it be possible for the Instituto to offer a full range of academic secondary courses. Nevertheless, as illiteracy had long been a serious problem for Priego, the re-establishment of an Instituto represented a significant step forward.[199]

In 1953 and 1954, two other institutions were opened, also of great value to the community. The Fundación Arjona Valera, created in 1947 as a result of a bequest by Doña Adelaida Arjona Castillo, opened its home for the elderly in the Avenida de España, and the Fundación Mármol, likewise a charitable organisation, established its residential centre looking out onto the church and old convent of San Francisco.

In a different way, three aspects of popular culture bear witness to the dynamism of the Priego community during these middle years of the twentieth century. The first, a clear indication of the increased spending power now available, is the inauguration at the end of the 1950s of a third cinema, the 'Cine Gran Capitán', with 1,200 seats, in addition to the 'Cine Victoria' and the 'Teatro Principal', which had stood in El Palenque since the 1840s. The second is the fact that Priego's bullring was the scene of as many as six or seven series of bullfights each year. And the third and perhaps most striking is the success enjoyed during the early 1960s of the town's football team, 'Atlético

---

[199] Osuna Luque, 96, points out that as late as 1991 the level of illiteracy in the Priego area remained above average for the province, notably among those aged above thirty.

Prieguense', which achieved promotion to the Third Division of the National League in 1961. It remained there for three seasons until poor business decisions and growing debt led to its disappearance from the national scene. That Priego's team rose to relative heights, albeit for just a few years, is a reflection of the town's status and prosperity at that time. It is equally true, however, that the sudden downturn in the club's fortunes coincided with a rapid decline in the industrial performance and economy of the town as a whole.[200]

La Plaza de la Constitución, popularly known as El Paseíllo. This had previously been the site of the Clarissan convent. The photograph was taken in the second decade of the twentieth century and published as a postcard by Castañeira y Álvarez, Madrid.

---

[200] Forcada Serrano, 2017, 128–29, charts the rise and fall of 'Atlético Prieguense' and its relationship with the town's prominence as an industrial centre.

Priego's town hall (El Ayuntamiento) and the Plaza de la Constitución in 2023
Photograph by Antonio Jesús Villena.

The present-day visitor to Priego might be surprised by the picture of Priego in the 1950s and the early 1960s as a thriving industrial centre, outstanding in this respect among the towns of Andalucía. This, however, is the image which for a time it was able to project. Alongside the producers of olive oil, the cotton mills continued to prosper and provide the basis for a generally prosperous community. There was still belief in the potential for further technological development and expansion and hope that a future rail link could radically reduce transport costs. Priego was indeed a colossus, but the perceptive observer could see that it had feet of clay.[201]

---

[201] Forcada Serrano, op. cit., 131.

II: Decline

The establishment of the new factory of Hilaturas del Carmen S.A. by José Linares Montero in 1957 opened up exciting new possibilities for Priego's cotton industry. Linares Montero had convinced the cotton ginning company CEPANSA that its new centre for the production of cotton yarn was to be situated in Priego, and by the beginning of 1960 this had opened with sixty-six employees, a figure which by 1963 had risen to 227. The expectation was that the ready availability of the cotton spinning industry's essential raw material would bring the town increased opportunities and further increase the possibilities for employment.

The economic background was changing, however, and the year 1959 is usually identified with a U-turn in the policy of Franco's government, embodied in the so-called 'Stabilisation Plan'. On the one hand, a package of deflationary measures led to a marked slowdown in the economy, affecting both employment and income and forcing inefficient companies to close. On the other hand, the policy of autarky (emphasising national economic self-reliance) was abandoned; Spain's very high tariff barriers were reduced and foreign capital could now be freely invested in Spanish industry. As a result, the conditions which had played so important a part in Priego's post-war boom ceased to exist. In addition, Spaniards were now allowed, and even encouraged, to seek work abroad. The last of these factors was to prove particularly significant for Priego as workers from both the villages and the urban area, whose welfare was now threatened by both factory closures and the mechanisation of agriculture, began to find employment in France, Germany and elsewhere.

The situation was further worsened by the Ministry of Agriculture's decision in 1962 to end the concessionary system that had underpinned the success of companies like CEPANSA and to ease restrictions on the importing of cotton. In the face of cheaper imports, the amount of cotton produced in Spain was radically reduced over the following decade.

By the end of 1966, CEPANSA, faced with a sharp decrease in the demand for cotton yarn, had produced a plan for restructuring the work of its factory, shifting the emphasis away from the production of yarn and onto weaving, in an attempt to preserve the current level of employment. It hurriedly set about installing 140 looms without waiting for official permission, an act which provoked a furious backlash and a legal challenge from the owners of other factories in Priego. Amidst accusations and counter-accusations of inefficiency and unwillingness to modernise, the dispute dragged on. Finally, in March 1968, it was resolved in favour of CEPANSA, whose transformation into a producer of both yarn and woven cotton (with 144 automatic looms) was now declared entirely legal. The company was to survive for a further decade, but its decline already appeared inevitable.

Warning voices had been raised as early as the end of the previous decade, pointing out the need for concerted action and modernisation of both equipment and business practices and drawing attention to the dangers posed by lack of vision for the future.[202] In spite of the commercial success being enjoyed by Priego's textile industry at its height, the perceptive observer could already detect signs of difficulty ahead: lack of expertise and commitment among a number of the mill owners and some workers and an absence of structure and organisation in the sector as a whole.[203]

In 1961, a group of seventeen of Priego's cotton mill owners agreed to amalgamate into one single business, thus increasing output but reducing the size of the workforce by over two thirds

---

[202] See, for example, the comments made by Pablo Gámiz Luque in 1959 in an article in *Adarve*, quoted by Forcada Serrano, 2017, 145–46.

[203] Matilla Rivadeneyra, 68–69.

(to a maximum of one hundred). The owners were to become shareholders or even employees of the new company. A number of other companies, however, intended to remain outside the scheme: some, the biggest of which were Textil el Carmen and Hijo y Viuda de Pedro Morales (each with over 120 employees), had already undertaken programmes of modernisation. Others planned to do so independently.

By 1963, sixteen of the original seventeen business owners had submitted a revised plan by which, with state aid (which would be a crucial factor), they hoped to protect existing jobs and even create sixty new ones. However, over the following three years, bureaucratic delays and a series of financial disputes between the employers and the national workers' organisation sapped confidence in the project. The Department of Industry set up an interministerial work group to examine Priego's difficulties but by May 1966 only four of the group of businesses were continuing to function. Members of the Priego council met with government officials, identifying the key problems to be resolved, but, following a further period of inaction, belief in the scheme for amalgamation and collaboration slipped away. It was finally abandoned in 1967. Although workers were inclined to blame the stubbornness and ineptitude of the employers, there is convincing evidence that the failure of this enterprise and the consequent ruin of Priego's cotton industry had more to do with broken promises and obstructiveness on the part of the Ministry, under pressure from the powerful Catalan industrialists.[204]

The implications of this failure for the people of Priego were considerable. In late 1967, the findings of a government survey of the businesses still operating in Priego were published in what was known as the Zafra report. This gave little hope for the future, within the present structure, for the workers whose jobs were under immediate threat. It did, however, make a number of recommendations for the future, of which the most enticing was

---

[204] Forcada Serrano, op. cit., 160–61.

the establishment of a cooperative for the production of clothing products using the textiles produced by the town's factories. This, it was hoped, would absorb the workforce left unemployed as a result of the closures. In spite of a hesitant response from Priego's factory owners, by February 1968, an extensive study had been produced by the local textile union, envisaging a daily output of 5,000 shirts, which would make use of 70% of the cotton fabric produced by the town's factories. Over the following years there were to be various initiatives attempting to seize this opportunity but, as will be seen in the following chapter, the dream was never to come true.

Between 1966 and 1972, twenty-six of Priego's cotton mills had closed. The official figure for the number of redundancies between 1960 and 1972 is 755, although the actual number was probably considerably higher. Various attempts at restructuring ultimately proved ineffective. Underlying causes for the failure of the industry include Priego's location, remote from the areas where cotton was produced and machinery was manufactured; failure to develop and modernise; excessive competition among several manufacturers all producing the same types of cloth; deficiencies with regard to dyeing and finishing; the difficulty of competing with companies in other parts of Spain; excessive production; the introduction of synthetic fibres and the increase in salaries.[205] In the face of this broad range of problems, no efforts by factory owners, the town council or workers' representatives could stop the sharp decline.

The crisis in the textile industry was, moreover, accompanied by a period of radical change in the agriculture of the area, which aggravated the unemployment problems that the crisis produced. The age of the horse and the donkey was giving way to that of the tractor and, in general, mechanisation of agricultural processes was reducing markedly the size of the workforce that was required in rural areas. Other industries

---

[205] Forcada Serrano analyses in detail the course and the causes of this decline: *op.cit.*, 171.

(such as those based on wood, pottery and metal) suffered badly, too. Ironically, the problems being encountered in Priego – as elsewhere in Andalucía – coincided with the economic boom being experienced in other parts of Spain, the so-called 'economic miracle' – and the result was a rapidly increasing rate of emigration from both urban Priego and the surrounding villages, notably to the industrialised areas of Cataluña as well as to other European countries. Between 1950 and 1981, Priego's population decreased by 28%.

In June 1966, *Adarve* published a lament for the town's textile industry written by the local poet Manuel Muñoz Jurado, which gave forceful expression to the consequences of the closures for the town and its people:

Se disipa como un sueño	As if it were a dream
la economía local	our economy fades away,
las fábricas de tejidos	and into ruin
van todas a liquidar.	fall the mills.
Es agobiante el problema	Crippling is the ill
en la industria del telar	of the industry of the loom,
que ampara cientos de obreros	once protector of hundreds
que van al paro total.	now without hope of work.
Si esto Dios no lo remedia	Without God's aid,
¿Dónde vamos a parar?	what fate awaits us?
Se queda paralizada	Robbed of life
la vida de la ciudad.	lies our town,
Porque la industria textil	for textiles
es obra tradicional	have always been
y, para orgullo de Priego,	Priego's pride,
la columna vertebral.	her backbone.
Este engranaje económico	Motor of the economy,
repercute por igual	its effects are everywhere;
y abarca todas las cosas	it takes in everything,
y ramos en general.	every part of life:
Ya que el obrero textil	the workers in the mills
cuando cobra su jornal	with their daily wage
le presta vida al comercio	give life to trade,

a la industria y al hogar.	industry and home.
Se va notando la crisis	Crisis appears
en las tiendas y en el bar,	in shops, the bar,
en los Bancos, en las Cajas	in banks; where we save
y en la plaza de comprar.	and where we spend.
Las fábricas que han quedado,	So too the mills that remain
que hacen por el mismo camino,	descend that same path,
camino de sucumbir.	the path to surrender.
Triste queda la ciudad	Wretched is our town,
sobre un ambiente sin vida	its spirit lifeless,
rodeada de amarguras,	encompassed by bitterness,
ahogada y empobrecida.	stifled, destitute.
Ya se oyen las campanas	In sadness now the bells
tocando tristes al duelo.	ring out a death knell,
Hay cuatro cirios candentes	with four burning candles
y un ataúd en el suelo.	and on the ground a coffin.
Ya la esquela mortuoria	The notice of death
se reparte por el pueblo	passes round the town
en letras negras grabadas	engraved in black,
oliendo a tinta de muerto.	smelling of dead man´s ink.
Falleció sin resistencia	Without a struggle it died,
una riqueza modelo	a model of prosperity,
dejando a los tantos años,	leaving after so many years
desconsolado recuerdo.	a melancholy memory.
Los obreros, hijos suyos,	The workers, its family,
la acompañan al sepelio	go with it to the grave
la huerta palacio abajo,	down through Huerta Palacio.[206]
camino del cementerio.	Down to the cemetery.
La condución del cadáver	The corpse was ready
estaba ya preparada	to be taken, from the time
al ver la concentración,	of the amalgamation,
que no sirve para nada.	which brings no gain.
Casi todos los esfuerzos	Almost every effort
para salvarla falló.	to save it failed.
Entre todos la mataron	Among them all they killed it
y ella sola se murió.	and alone it died.
Lloran los trabajadores	The workers weep

---

[206] The Huerta Palacio is an outlying district of Priego.

pidiendo clemencia al cielo:	begging heaven's mercy,
porque han perdido su pan,	having lost their daily bread
ganado con tanto celo.	won with such ardour.
El entierro es imponente	The burial is full of sorrow
que solo afecta al obrero;	for the worker alone,
y el ataúd es enorme,	but the coffin is vast
porque pilla todo el pueblo.	and swallows all the town.
¿Quién va dentro de la caja	Who is in that box
que despide tanto fuego?	which gives off such fire?
Una industria que ha cesado.	An industry which is no more.
La industria Textil de Priego.	Priego's textile industry.
Cuando ya no se fabriquen	When 'chester', 'paten'
chester ni paten ni lona,	and canvas are made no more,
tendrán los trabajadores	workers will have to
que emigrar para otra zona.	go and live elsewhere.
Aquí no hay na que rascar,	Here there's naught to be had,
Aquí la bolsa no sona.	no money to be made.
¡¡Hay que coger las maletas,	So let's pack our bags;
y tirar pa Barcelona!!	we're off to Barcelona!

For the people of Priego, it was indeed the end of an era.

CHAPTER 9
Meeting New Challenges

∽

I: A town transformed

General Franco's death in November 1975 marked the beginning of a period of profound change which overtook many aspects of Spanish society. The whole of the nation felt the effects of the social and political transformation which began to take place between the early tentative steps towards compromise and reconciliation and the eventual election of Felipe González's socialist government – with its strong Andalusian base – in 1982. Priego de Córdoba was no exception, although inevitably it was some way from experiencing the heady enthusiasm and optimism felt by many, and especially the young, in the major urban centres. Priego continued to face severe economic problems in the wake of the collapse of the textile industry, it had limited facilities for public welfare (it possessed, for example, no hospital or health centre) and in 1975 conditions in some of the villages remained primitive. The population had fallen, notably through emigration to Cataluña. Democracy brought a sense of optimism, but for many this was soon to be stifled by more immediate practical concerns.

Like many Spanish towns, Priego was quick to remove the superficial trappings of Franco's regime. One sign of this was the changes made in street names. La Calle Héroes de Toledo (commemorating the defence by Franco's supporters of Toledo's *alcázar*) now became la Calle Río, and la Calle José Antonio (named after the founder of the Falange) and la Plaza del General Franco became la Calle Carrera de las Monjas and la

Plaza de Andalucía respectively. La Calle Ribera ceased to bear the name of the fearsome General Queipo de Llano, and la Calle del 18 de Julio (celebrating the beginning of the Nationalist uprising against the Republic) acquired the equally significant title of la Calle de la Libertad.

With regard to the town's economy, there were early signs of enthusiasm. For example, an editorial in *Adarve* written in July 1976 praises the energy and initiative of the young entrepreneurs who were giving the town a new life: 'Textile factories and those producing articles of clothing, yarn and knitted goods are like hives buzzing from dawn to dusk, transforming the past tragedy into a breath of hope and optimism.'[207] Encouraging indeed, although in the long term the belief in the revival of the town's textile industry was to prove largely misplaced. Six months later, *Adarve*'s editorial was to lament the provincial authority's decision to exclude Priego from its Industrial Expansion Plan.[208] The last of the textile mills closed over the following few years: La Textil Campera, for example, functioned only intermittently after 1981 and it finally closed its doors in the mid-1980s. Textil del Carmen, which in its day had been the largest company in the history of Priego, by 1977 had just six employees and was sold and adapted to clothing manufacture. Texruiz SL, the last Priego company to install cutting-edge technology in an attempt to combine the production of modern textiles with that of clothing manufactured in its own factory, did indeed continue to operate as a family-run enterprise until the beginning of 2004. It then finally succumbed to the pressure created by imported clothing produced in China, elsewhere in Asia and in Africa.

'La confección', clothing manufacture, was for several years the focus of Priego's hopes to replace the textile mills as a source of employment. A study carried out at the beginning of the 1980s showed that, out of Priego's total of almost 20,000 inhabitants,

---

[207] *Adarve*, 15.7.76, p.3.

[208] *Adarve*, 15.1.77, p.1.

524 were employed in clothing manufacture by thirty-two companies.[209] These were by no means, however, all full-time jobs. Seasonal variations dictated by the availability of stock meant that some workers had employment for only part of the year; the number of permanent full-time workers was relatively low. A large proportion of the employees were women, many of whom worked from home. Such enterprises involved a low level of capital investment, and the sector was characterised by the rapid birth and demise of small companies.[210] The benefits for the community as a whole could never be comparable with those that had previously been provided by the cotton mills, and the employment provided could not make up for the jobs that had been lost. Nevertheless, this industry was seen as one of the pillars which could support the local economy, both in Priego itself and in the rural areas, taking advantage of the availability of very cheap labour.[211]

Priego began to broaden its horizons. By the early 1980s, the town was beginning to view in a positive light its connections with Cataluña – in terms both of the links that now existed with the *prieguenses* who had settled there and of the commercial ties that existed as a result of the clothing trade. The town council made strenuous efforts to encourage the clothing industry, and from 1988 an annual fair was organised to promote its products, which attracted increasing numbers of visitors. From 1992, this was complemented by an annual design competition. The following few years were to see a drop in sales, however, and, although it was felt that Priego's business owners had by now gained in experience and expertise, the problems that the industry faced would soon become increasingly apparent. By the end of the decade, the number of companies participating in the fair was dropping markedly. Strenuous efforts were made to market Priego's products abroad through attendance at

---

[209] Sánchez López et al., p.35.
[210] Ibid., 30–32.
[211] Ibid., 109–10.

international trade fairs, and in 2001 the town council made available a site in the La Vega industrial estate for the establishment of a Technological Textile Centre. It was some years before this centre finally took shape, however, and in the meantime it became more and more obvious that Priego would struggle to compete in a market dominated by cheaply produced foreign goods, especially from China. By the end of 2006, *Adarve* reported that the town's economy was paralysed, with its textile sector 'in a permanent state of crisis' as a result of foreign competition.[212]

Fortunately, on the other hand, the agricultural sector had been faring much better, specifically in terms of the production and marketing of olive oil. The industry had long been firmly established in and around Priego, and the cooperative La Purísima, for instance, had been founded as a pioneering enterprise as early as 1945. On 1st January 1986, Spain had acquired the status of a fully-fledged member of the European Community, which in 1992 became the European Union. Membership brought considerable benefits for Spanish agriculture, not least the aid that the Common Agricultural Policy provided for the owners of small farms. There were other far-reaching changes taking place in Priego's rural areas: by the 1980s, some of those who had moved to other parts of Spain were beginning to return, bringing money to invest. Others who left their village each summer to work in the tourist industry, notably in Mallorca, brought back their profits and used a significant part of them to purchase substantial areas of olive groves. The industry was rapidly being re-energised. Olive trees had long been a prominent feature of the rural landscape, but by now large areas of land which in the past had been given over to arable farming were being devoted to the production of what was being viewed as liquid gold.

In 1992, a record harvest coincided with the provisional approval of the *denominación de origen* for the olive oils of the

---

[212] *Adarve*, 15/31.12.2006, p.6.

Priego area.[213] From the point of view of marketing and the recognition of the product's qualities, this was a crucial step forward. In the same year, the Priego company Mueloliva was ranked 18th among Andalucía's food-producing companies. Progress was not entirely uniform: in 1995, on account of an extended period of drought, the yield was one of the worst on record, and the following year a steep increase in price caused a drop in consumption and a protest of alarmed farmers in Brussels. Nevertheless, the *denominación de origen* was now fully approved, and an award in Germany pointed to the opening up of a new market in that country. 1998 saw a wave of protest by the producers against the quota initially introduced by the European Union, but this was finally increased to 700,000 tonnes. Half a dozen brands of oil were now being marketed under Priego's *denominación de origen*, and one from the Cooperative of El Cañuelo received an award from the Ministry of Agriculture. There was now much closer collaboration over marketing among Priego's cooperatives, but it was recognised that in terms of the commercialisation of its products the area still had a great deal to learn from the Italians.

If the production of olive oil and clothing manufacture continued to be considered the twin pillars on which Priego's economy rested, it was becoming increasingly clear that it was the former that carried greater hope for the future. In 2001, under the auspices of the *denominación de origen*, seven of the area's oil-producing cooperatives joined forces to market their oil under the name of Almazaras de la Subbética, opening its headquarters and shop in Priego. The following year, Mueloliva strengthened its position in the market by acquiring the distributing company Minerva. Priego's extra virgin olive oils continued to harvest prestigious awards, and in 2003, the area's own annual prize competition was launched as part of a week of

---

[213] *Denominación de origen* is a labelling system that regulates the quality of Spanish foodstuffs. There is a semi-autonomous governing body for each region and for each food type, which investigates the quality, ingredients and production process for each product, ensuring that specific quality levels are maintained.

celebration of their qualities. 2005 saw a wide range of national and international successes with the area's large number of small producers playing an important role; efficiency and yields were increased through the introduction of new machinery and improved treatments for the olive trees.

The one dark cloud on the horizon was the suspected scandal surrounding the dealings of the company Almazaras de Priego, which had accumulated a deficit of some ten million euros, inflicting heavy losses on about 2,000 families. Over the year 2004–05, Almazaras had made only 1.4 euros per kilo of oil, while the generally accepted price was between three and four euros. The families that had been affected took legal action and, as the case dragged on, the association that they had formed appealed to the Bank of Spain to investigate the company's dealings.

To the two existing pillars of its economy, Priego was keen to add a third: tourism. A combination of the attractiveness of the old town, the wealth of monumental Baroque architecture and the appeal of the surrounding countryside for rural tourism offered great hope for the future, to which *Adarve* gave confident expression in 1997:

> Tourism has begun to form part of Priego's economy. Day by day we are seeing more excursions to Priego and, although this is only a beginning, it is already making its contribution. With time, who knows whether income from tourism may represent a good percentage of the local economy. At present there are more and more restaurants opening their doors on a daily basis and this is already a good sign. Anyway, Priego should have its infrastructure and places in hotels ready in case tourism makes a real breakthrough.[214]

It was, however, already becoming clear that Priego, although it was increasingly successful in bringing in day visitors or those making short stays at weekends or on festival days, was

---

[214] *Adarve*, 15.12.1997, p.4.

likely to find it much more difficult to attract the longer-term visits which would bring real benefit to its economy and create a significant amount of employment. The early years of the new century saw strenuous efforts to promote Priego's image as a tourist destination: increased attendance at fairs and conferences, the establishment of a new association linking hotels, rural accommodation and restaurants, the opening in 2004 of the four-star hotel Huerta de las Palomas, and in the following year the establishment of a new tourist office in the town centre. At the same time, a new strategic plan under the title 'Vive la Experiencia' ('Live the Experience') was set out, and the first National Tourist Communication and Marketing Conference was also held in Priego. All of this should have produced a real sense of progress, but, although statistics pointed to an increase in the number of visitors, hotel owners continued to lament the small number of overnight stays. Further initiatives followed, such as the 'Tourism and Oil' project, which generated gastronomic events attended by well-known professionals. In spite of energetic and enterprising efforts at marketing, somehow Priego's tourist sector was not quite taking off. One explanation given was that the town's monuments were usually visited in half a day, partly on account of the limited opening times of the churches. Some tourists complained, as they still do, about practical problems such as the difficulty of car parking.

*

The final decades of the twentieth century witnessed something of a recovery in the size of Priego's population. In 1981, the number of inhabitants of the town together with the villages stood at 19,485, but a decade later this figure had risen to over 21,000. In addition, there was a steady flow of population from the countryside into the town. In consequence, the urban area continued to expand, most notably along the east-west axis represented by Calle Ramón y Cajal and the Avenida de España. New suburbs cut into what had previously been rural land. The town's growth did not, however, benefit from a coherent and logical strategy. An evaluation of its progress published in 1993 pointed to the absence of a clearly defined urban structure, resulting from inadequate planning combined with the difficulties caused by the irregularity of the terrain, with some districts poorly connected to the rest of the town. The same article laments various other deficiencies in the town's recent development, notably those resulting from the inadequacies of the road system and also the poor provision in terms of essential services. In addition, its author criticises the harm that had been done to the town's architectural heritage, such as the destruction of the remains of the church of Santiago, next to the castle, the stretch of the old wall next to the Arch of Santa Ana and much of the traditional Andalusian housing, and he also draws attention to what he considers to be the insensitive remodelling of the Plaza del Llano next to the church of La Asunción.[215]

On the other hand, the article points to an increase in spending on public projects in recent years and to the more rigorous controls now being imposed on urban development.[216] The most obvious need that had to be addressed in the late 1970s was the absence of a hospital or adequate medical facility. After extensive campaigning, in 1981, confirmation was finally obtained from the Ministry of Health that funding was to be made available for the construction of a new health centre on the site of what had been a football pitch near the centre of the town. The new centre was finally opened in 1985, although there was disappointment at the level of both the facilities and the staffing. Twenty years later, there were still protests about the deficiencies in the centre and the insufficient funding available. The Andalusian authorities turned a deaf ear to the pleas for the

---

[215] Vera Aranda, p.153–54, 156–57.

[216] Ibid., p.52.

establishment of a hospital in Priego; critics pointed out that few towns with a population of 20,000 or more had fewer medical facilities and that the situation was made worse by the fact that Priego's population was distributed throughout over twenty villages. In 2008, the available budget was so limited that staff absences could not be covered, and it was argued that three doctors were doing the work of eight. In the same year, the centre's air conditioning broke down and, in spite of 40° heat, it could not be repaired.

Nevertheless, in other respects, there was undeniable progress. Also in 1985 a new post office was opened and work began on the construction of the new bus station, where the town prison had previously stood and a very short distance from the health centre. In addition, a site was identified for a development of cheap social housing. In the years which followed, a raft of prestigious projects took shape, such as the establishment of a new home for the elderly (1996); the opening of an adult education centre (1989); the establishment in 1990 of the Albasur association for the disabled, eventually with its own premises (begun in 1999); the rebuilding and enlargement of the Residencia Arjona Valera (first announced by the Foundation in 2003); and the construction of the municipal sports complex (subsequently remodelled, extended, equipped with an all-weather surface, and reopened in 2003 as the 'Ciudad Deportiva Priego') and also of the sports hall known as the Pabellón de Deportes (opened in 1992) near the eastern entry to the town. Probably the most ambitious project was the development of the central Palenque area, initially announced in 1993 but not completed for well over a decade because of lack of funding. This included extensive municipal offices and eventually a new public library (opened in 2007). The Palenque complex also included a Mercadona supermarket with an underground car park. Other important developments included the establishment of the municipal park and exhibition centre named after Niceto Alcalá-Zamora (extended in 1995) and of the

Arts Pavilion (first used in 2000).[217] The Teatro Victoria was purchased, refurbished, modernised and re-opened in 1999. Essential work on the town's infrastructure included the completion of the task of canalising the river water and resurfacing numerous streets, and notably that of the improvement of drainage and subsequent repaving carried out (not without controversy) in the iconic Barrio de la Villa. The remodelling of the Plaza de Andalucía in the centre of the town and the adjoining Calle Ribera was completed in 1995. By 2004, planning was underway for the new *mercado de abastos,* or indoor food market, next to the church of San Pedro and on the site of the old Alcantarine (Franciscan) convent. In 2003, building projects in the town's schools were announced, to the value of six million euros. There were plans (first presented in 2001) for a new civil guard barracks to be built at the western end of the town; by the beginning of the new century, work was underway on the extensive new housing development, Los Almendros, situated in the same area. In addition, important work was done on several of Priego's monumental buildings, such as the restoration of the chapel of El Calvario and its esplanade, the setting for the culminating events of the Good Friday processions. And in terms of Priego's commercial life, a crucial step forward was the creation in the early 1990s of the industrial estate at La Vega, situated on the road leading towards Las Angosturas, to the north-east of the town.

---

[217] By the 1970s, the nature of the traditional September fair had changed markedly. It was no longer essentially the occasion for the sale and exchange of livestock which had brought large numbers of villagers with their animals into town. Indeed, the breeding of livestock was now much less important for the local rural economy. The new fairground now offered a place for festivities characterised by music, dance and the display of finery. In 1980, the Agropriego festival, devoted to agricultural machinery and plant protection products, took place for the first time. It, too, was to become an annual event, held about two weeks after the *feria.* It was still flourishing over forty years later, with over one hundred exhibitors.

The public library
In 2003, the town council took possession of the 'Edificio Palenque', which had been built in the Plaza del Palenque by the Mercadona supermarket chain; but it was another two years before the library, which occupies the third floor of part of the complex of municipal buildings, could be opened to the public. *Photograph by Antonio Jesús Villena.*

This list of improvements made to Priego's facilities and infrastructure, embracing a wide range of aspects of the everyday life of the community, is far from comprehensive, but it does give a sense of the steps which the town was taking to modernise and to improve the quality of life of its citizens over the first three decades of the post-Franco era. There were many delays and frustrations, but the extent of the achievement is undeniable. The funds available for this expenditure had grown steadily. By 1984, the municipal budget had risen to 243 million pesetas (approximately 1.46 million euros), and within a decade this figure was to increase six-fold. At the same time, however, there was growing concern about the level of municipal debt, which over the following years was to grow apace.[218]

The church of San Pedro and the indoor food market
The church formed part of the convent founded in 1664 by the 'alcantarinos' (a branch of the Franciscans) and was completed in 1683. A food market was built in 1905 on what had been the site of the convent cloister, but it did not survive beyond the middle of the century. However, in 2016, a new building, containing offices, a market and a car park, was opened in the same space to meet obvious needs. *Photograph by Antonio Jesús Villena.*

The provision of new and improved facilities also extended to the villages, for example, with the opening of sports centres in Castil de Campos and Zamoranos in 1992. In the years which followed, Castil de Campos continued to take striking initiatives; 1996 saw the inauguration of its museum of rural

---

[218] By 2009, Priego's public debt would reach over 13.5 million euros, a disconcerting figure, although certainly not exceptional among Andalusian towns.

life and two years later it obtained permission to open a pharmacy. More conspicuously, it sought and obtained authorisation to become an *entidad local autónoma*, thus gaining the right to its own *ayuntamiento* or village council. In 1995, the hotel complex known as *la villa turística de Priego* was opened in the village of Zagrilla and subsequently the mycological garden 'La Trufa', specialising in Andalusian fungi, was established nearby.

At a more fundamental level, much-needed work on the infrastructure of Priego's outlying communities had steadily been taking place since the 1970s, including the improvement of road surfaces, the laying of pavements and the installation of piping for drainage and for the provision of domestic water. It should be pointed out that in some of the smaller villages conditions had long remained primitive, with electricity not available in some cases until the end of the 1960s and no mains water until about 1980. Equally important progress was now made in terms of the quality of the access roads, which in the new century was to open up the villages to a further wave of changes, among them an influx of new residents: the much more comfortable conditions coupled with greatly improved communications now made the area an attractive one for immigrants from northern Europe.

Indeed, throughout Priego's history, difficulty of access had severely affected the town's social and economic progress. Not only was there no railway but also connections by road had been poor. In 1985, plans were published for the construction of a new road to connect Priego with Lucena and Cabra to the west and Alcalá la Real to the east. *Adarve* waxed lyrical about the prospects:

> A connecting road of this kind is of the utmost importance for solving the problem of the east-west link and for improving the level of accessibility for the Priego-Alcalá la Real area, at present considered the worst in all of Andalucía. The improvement in communication will mean that our town can overcome its age-old

isolation, with enormous possibilities being opened up for it in all sectors, but above all in that of tourism.[219]

Early progress was encouraging, but work slowed, and eight years later there was speculation about whether the project would be completed by the end of the century.[220] The doubts were indeed justified and in 2005 *Adarve* was still expressing bitter criticism of the Andalusian government for allowing the project to drag on unfinished.[221]

*

A particularly striking feature of Priego's development in the early decades of the post-Franco period is the considerable effort – and expense – devoted to reinforcing the town's awareness of its own distinctive cultural identity. This took on a rich variety of forms. The opening of the *Peña flamenca* in 1980, with the help of funding provided by the town council, the religious brotherhoods and a number of the town's businesses, was laden with promise for the future. Year after year, a varied offering of musical events enlivened Priego's cultural calendar, and among its outstanding features were the blossoming international career of the soprano Carmen Serrano and the creation of the town's symphonic orchestra in 2005.

1999 saw the opening of the Museo Adolfo Lozano Sidro, which displayed numerous works by Priego's distinguished artist as well as providing a home for the town's Museum of Municipal History. The same year witnessed the commemoration of the fiftieth anniversary of the death of Niceto Alcalá-Zamora, now viewed with pride as Priego's most famous son, and also the re-opening to the public of the newly refurbished house in Calle Río in which he had been born and grew up.[222]

---

[219] *Adarve*, 15.12.85, p.3.

[220] *Adarve*, 15.12.93, p.7.

[221] *Adarve*, 15/31.12. 2005, p.7.

[222] The house had been donated to the town by Alcalá-Zamora's family in 1986 and initially opened to the public in 1987.

Priego now confidently regarded itself as the cultural capital of the Subbética region. It had long been outstanding, of course, as a centre for Baroque art, and this was reflected in the hosting, in 1984, of a summer course on this subject. The town's range of cultural interests was much wider, however. Once again, we can look to *Adarve*, in this case its review of 1996, to capture the sense of pride in the range and quality of Priego's achievement.

> Culture was omnipresent throughout the year, with a long list of activities and events, including the following: the second Symposium on Alcalá-Zamora and his times; the first Exhibition of Young People´s Art; the thirteenth year of the Ángel Carrillo Literary Competition; the ninth Landscape Painting course; the third Exhibition of Popular Arts and Customs; the eighth Spring Musical week; the second Summer Course on Franciscanism; the Summer Cultural Programme; the forty-ninth Festival of Music, Theatre and Dance; the nineteenth Flamenco Festival; and a more extensive list of exhibitions, conferences, etc., which mark us out as the town in our province with the greatest number of cultural events.[223]

To this should be added the establishment of a rapidly growing number of associations – cultural, sporting, professional, charitable, health-related, and also an active and prestigious mycological society – which were to become an increasingly prominent feature of the town's life.

A particularly striking feature of this period was the conspicuous effort that Priego made to explore and chart its own historical development. The Museum of Municipal History, which had initially been established in 1983 in the Carnicerías Reales, was reopened at the end of the 1990s in what is now the Adolfo Lozano Sidro Cultural Centre. The appointment of the archaeologist Rafael Carmona as director of the museum was a

---

[223] *Adarve*, 15/31.12.96, p.6. The annual Landscape Painting Course, for example, involved such distinguished artists as Antonio Zarco, Antonio Povedano and Luis García Ochoa and the sculptor Venancio Blanco.

crucial one, and in the ensuing years he went on to oversee a wealth of important discoveries, including those relating to the prehistoric, Hispano-Roman and Islamic periods as well as the fortifications of medieval Christian Priego. This work was chronicled in the prestigious journal *Antiquitas*, first published in 1990. There were evident frustrations, as when in 1996 the Ibero-Roman fortifications were destroyed by the landowner, even though he was well informed about their importance.[224] On the other hand, there were exciting discoveries that provided valuable information on the town's origins, most notably that of the remains of the Roman villa under the courtyard of the Colegio de las Angustias in the very centre of Priego.

In 1998, the historical journal *Legajos* appeared for the first time, under the auspices of the municipal archive and edited by Jesús Cuadros, and throughout this period a considerable body of highly informed and scholarly work, covering numerous facets of the town's history and culture, was published by historians of the quality of Manuel Peláez del Rosal, Miguel Forcada Serrano and Enrique Alcalá Ortiz. Their prolific output represents an important facet of Priego's vigorous effort to celebrate its rich and varied cultural history, and it is with justification that the pages of *Adarve* were able to ring out their praise for the 'period of cultural splendour being experienced in the town'.[225]

And in a particularly conspicuous respect, Priego continued to preserve some of its oldest and most representative features. It might have been expected that, given the more liberal – and increasingly secular – values which characterised much of Spanish society in the post-Franco period, the importance attached by the town's people to displays of Christian devotion and specifically to the brotherhoods and *cofradías* would have declined. In fact, this proved to be far from the case. The socialist councils of the late 1970s and early 1980s imposed no constraints

---

[224] *Adarve*, 15.12.96/1.1.97, p.7.

[225] *Adarve*, 15/31.12.2002, p.6.

on the activities of these bodies, except for very minor episodes such as the prohibition in 1980 by the mayor Pedro Sobrados of the launching of rockets and the making of excessive noise after midnight. The *cofradías*, seen as an expression of popular tradition and religious fervour, went from strength to strength. In ten years, five new brotherhoods were founded and yet more followed, for example, la Hermandad del Rocío ('Brotherhood of the Dew'), which burst onto the scene in 1989, and the Hermandad de Nuestro Padre Jesús en la Oración en el Huerto y María Santísima de la Paz ('Brotherhood of Our Father Jesus at Prayer in the Garden and the Holiest Mary of Peace'), founded in 2004. The hierarchy of the brotherhoods had understood well the need for the democratisation of their structures and for the members of the social elites who had dominated them to make way for people from other sectors of society. In addition, women were now able to participate in their activities on a level equal with men. In 1990, the Hermandad de Belén ('Brotherhood of Bethlehem') became the first to elect a woman to its highest office. Miguel Forcada describes the immense effort which went into the work of the brotherhoods over these years as 'a magnificent display of popular religiosity'.[226]

II: Crisis once again

Priego de Córdoba was far from alone in finding itself plunged into economic difficulty in the years which followed the international financial crash of 2008. In Spain, the effects of the crisis were not felt immediately, but when they arrived they were intensified by the bursting of the country's 'property bubble'. It was not only the builders themselves who felt the direct effects but also the numerous workers in Priego and its villages, who depended on a variety of related trades: carpenters, plumbers, electricians, painters. Owners of small

---

[226] Forcada Serrano, 2000, p.356.

companies who had previously employed several workers now found themselves struggling to scrape a living or in several cases were driven out of business.

Negative consequences were soon felt, with the failure or abandonment of financial initiatives such as the scheme to build a commercial centre in the new housing development of Los Almendros. Other projects suffered frustrating delays, notably those affecting the completion of the now notorious A339. Important developments such as the indoor food market and the civil guard barracks showed no signs of coming to fruition. In 2010, *Adarve* reported that 'the local economy is still in a state of paralysis with not one sector enjoying a successful time'.[227] As in many parts of Spain, levels of unemployment reached unnervingly high levels, and prospects for many of the area's young people appeared bleak. A number of restaurants which had quite recently opened, believing in the wave of prosperity that tourism could bring, were now closing. Priego's clothing industry, in the face of a surge of cheap imported goods from China, had plummeted to a new low (a journalist described it as 'tilting at windmills'). It was the agricultural sector which effectively remained as the sole support of the area's economy. Even here, there were problems. Farmers complained bitterly at the low prices that they were paid: in 2008, the figure had fallen to just over two euros for a kilo of olive oil. In addition, the repercussions of the Almazaras de Priego scandal rumbled on, with prison sentences eventually handed out to those responsible.

Nevertheless, Priego's olive oil attracted more and more attention on the world stage, and international awards came thick and fast. In 2013, oils that were part of the area's *denominación de origen* won no fewer than 114 awards. In 2017, AOVEs (extra virgin olive oils) from the Priego region dominated the world rankings, winning seven of the ten top prizes awarded by the World Association of Journalists and

---

[227] *Adarve*, 15/31.12.2010, p.5.

Wine Writers. Three oils stand out: Venta del Barón (produced by Mueloliva), which in 2016 won an award as the best oil in the world for the fourth consecutive year, Knolive Epicure (best in the world in 2018) and the organic Rincón de la Subbética (Almazaras de la Subbética), which by 2023 had won over 500 prizes worldwide. The successes continued, although this did not put an end to the farmers' protests at the low prices that they were being paid: early in 2020, a vast demonstration involved the blocking of the A45 motorway.

Steadily, if timidly, the economic recovery began to make its effects felt. By 2015, the tourist sector was starting to show encouraging signs, benefitting from the tourist office's excellent new website and publicity material. Rural accommodation, hotels and restaurants were reporting the arrival of more visitors. By 2019, the total figure recorded had reached 33,357, although sadly this growth was again to be stunted by the pandemic.

Green projects were playing an increasingly prominent part in the council's policies. Following lengthy discussions with landowners, in June 2022 the pathway up the mountain of La Tiñosa was officially reopened, with the aim of bringing further development of rural tourism to areas such as the village of Las Lagunillas, where the new pathway would begin at an altitude of just over 800 metres. Within the town, 900,000 euros were made available for the installation of more energy-efficient lighting.

Steadily, too, a number of long-awaited municipal projects came to fruition. 2011 saw the inauguration of new secondary school, Carmen Pantión. By 2014, the industrial estate was being extended, and this process continued throughout the decade. Work began on the new civil guard barracks in 2015, and it finally came into operation in 2018–2019, having cost a total of 2,700,000 euros. The indoor food market finally opened in 2016, with the aid of a contribution of over a million euros made by the provincial *Diputación*. As part of the same site there was a suite of offices and meeting rooms, forming a new Centre for

Business Initiatives. The previous year had seen the opening of an extensive new centre for social services and also a heliport for use in medical emergencies. There continued to be complaints of marginalisation by the Andalusian government (the Junta de Andalucía) when in 2018 a new hospital was announced for Lucena while Priego's pleas for such a facility were again being ignored. On the other hand, by 2021, *Adarve* was writing warmly of the financial support that the regional authorities had made available for a number of municipal projects as well as for the improvement of roads.[228] The Junta had spent 3,100,000 euros on tackling the most hazardous stretches of the A339. Substantial sums continued to be invested in education and in 2022, the Junta de Andalucía contributed some four million euros to the improvement of Priego's schools.

Priego's biggest urban project, however, was the redevelopment of Calle Río, involving the installation of an extensive new drainage system. It was eventually completed in 2023. This vast enterprise created havoc for traffic and pedestrians alike and brought echoes of the difficulties caused by the similar work done in the same street a century before.

Priego continued to place considerable emphasis on cultural matters. In 2000, the council had announced the purchase of the mill owned by the Montoro-Castilla family for use as an archaeological-ethnographic museum; it was not until September 2022 that detailed plans were announced for the building's refurbishment, with the aid of 1,600,000 euros of funding from the Junta. Further delays were to follow as a result of financial pressures. The mill, when completed, is to form part of a complex of historic buildings running from the castle down towards the Carnicerías Reales. It should make possible the display of a much greater proportion of Priego's archaeological holdings than is at present the case.

The restoration of the castle, with its 13th–14th century keep, had already been completed, once again with funding from the

---

[228] *Adarve*, 15/31.12.21, p.5.

Junta, and just below it lay the historic gardens known originally as the Huerta de las Infantas and more recently as the Recreo de Castilla. Having fallen into a state of abandonment, these were acquired from the Castilla family, extensively restored (with the aid of European funding) and opened to the public in 2013.

In 2022, Priego celebrated the 150th anniversary of the birth of Adolfo Lozano Sidro with numerous exhibitions, lectures and concerts and the publication of a new study of his work. In the same year, the 90th anniversary of the proclamation of the Second Republic was similarly (though belatedly) commemorated through a series of exhibitions, lectures and publications. Priego was demonstrating that it could now look back on a period of division and conflict with clarity and objectivity.

Elsewhere, important restoration work continued, including in 2021 that of the altarpiece of La Asunción and in 2019 the (somewhat controversial) paving of the esplanade of El Calvario. There was also an extensive programme for the restoration of the Fuente del Rey, already underway. In 2022, the part of the Holy Week celebrations known as the *Prendimiento* (the representation of the seizure of Christ) was officially declared a heritage event of cultural interest by the Junta de Andalucía; the performances of the Brotherhood of La Aurora had also been proposed for the same distinction. The splendours of the celebrations of Holy Week, the May festival and Corpus Christi continued to be seen as a jewel in Priego's crown, and there could be no doubt that pride in the town's rich historical tradition remained a fundamental guiding principle in the formulation of its policies for the future. Tourism was clearly now viewed as providing a vital means of giving the town new energy and a sense of direction. Significantly, two new hotels both had close links with the town's history: the Hospedería San Francisco, opened in 2012, took full advantage of the highly attractive setting of the recently restored Franciscan convent, while the Hotel-Museo Patria Chica, closely associated with the Valverde family, opened its doors in 2017, taking its name from the journal founded by Carlos Valverde 102 years previously.

The number of social, cultural and sporting associations continued to grow rapidly. Priego promoted an increasingly wide range of sporting activities, and in 2021 and 2022 its representatives achieved national or regional distinction in marathon running, the walk event, motocross, karate and *padel*. Most significantly, the town has steadily consolidated its position as the nation's most prestigious centre for table tennis. This has much to do with the outstanding success of Priego-born Carlos Machado, who honed his skills as a member of the local team, CajaSur Priego TM, which has a highly distinguished record at national level. Machado has eleven times been Spanish national champion, seven of them consecutively, and he has also won the doubles championship in partnership with his brother José Luis. In 2022, José Luis continued Priego's domination of the sport by winning the National Veterans' trophy. The town's sports complex, the Ciudad Deportiva, now bears the name of Carlos Machado.

*

As Priego approached the end of the century's second decade, there were indeed optimistic signs for the future. In 2017, it was announced that the town was to receive a substantial grant from a European fund for urban development, and in 2020, plans were announced for the rehabilitation of the Atarazana district at the western end of the town, including the construction of a new sports and leisure centre.

Undoubtedly there were also serious difficulties still to be addressed. Although Priego escaped the worst ravages of the COVID pandemic, in its wake the town was left scarred by the closure of a growing number of small businesses. The 2020s were also a time for the town council to face up to one particularly deep-rooted problem. In 2010–11, it had entered into partnership with a private company – Aqualia – for the administration of the water supply to the town and villages. The jointly run business took the name Aguas de Priego. Within a year, there were numerous complaints with regard to its competence, and there were soon calls for the council to reassume control. Years of dry weather exacerbated the problems, but frustration mounted, with some villages still without drinkable water in their taps after several years. In July 2022, the council finally took the difficult decision to reassume total control over Aguas de Priego, and this, including the cost of paying off the substantial sum owed by the company, had the effect of almost doubling the municipal debt.

Priego had certainly been far from unique in experiencing radical changes over the previous half-century. Moreover, in the face of deeply troubling international developments, like very many other communities both in Spain and abroad, it now had to confront further financial, social and environmental challenges. In its favour it had an undeniably strong sense of cultural identity, and in the olive oil industry it possessed a major source of economic strength, but there were some disconcerting signs, too. To a considerable extent, Priego's present reflected a combination of pride in its past glories and a belief, seemingly well founded, in its traditional agricultural activities, but where did that leave its future?

Postscript: Priego Past, Present and Future

∽

> Time present and time past
> Are both perhaps present in time future,
> And time future contained in time past.
>
> T.S. Eliot

In 2020, Priego's town council produced a detailed report setting out the reasoning behind its Sustainable and Integrated Strategy for Urban Development (EDUSI). This extensive document lists what were perceived to be the problems and challenges facing the town, as well as its strengths and the opportunities for future development. The difficulties to be overcome included the inadequacy of communication by road; the distribution of trade; tourist activities and services in different parts of the town; the difficulties encountered in particular by the elderly in gaining access to the historical centre and the considerable practical problem of car parking; excessive dependence on the olive and olive oil industry (97% of the land under cultivation was given over to olive farming); failure to take sufficient advantage of the possibilities for new forms of tourism in rural areas, including in villages such as Castil de Campos, Zamoranos, Zagrilla, Esparragal and Lagunillas; the ageing population; poor accessibility for the disabled; failure to exploit renewable energy resources; the low standard of education, particularly among the elderly (in 2015, a staggering 24% of Priego's population was illiterate or had no educational qualifications as opposed to 13% in the province as a whole); ignorance, particularly in rural areas, of the opportunities offered by new technology; and a high level of unemployment (in 2016, this stood at 19.57%, higher than the neighbouring areas), especially among women.[229]

On the other hand, the report points to what its authors considered to be the area's significant strengths. Prominent among these is Priego's 'enterprising and entrepreneurial spirit'; the report mentions that it had been named Andalucía's most dynamic town by the journal *Andalucía Económica*. Unsurprisingly, this analysis also emphasises the highly developed agrifood sector and also Priego's great wealth in terms of culture and landscape, citing its recognition by the national newspaper *ABC* as 'Spain's prettiest town'. Considerable weight is placed on the potential for further development of facilities for tourism; and Priego's mycological garden and museum – the only one of its kind in Europe – receives particular attention.[230]

The report goes on to examine the opportunities which exist for future development, stressing the need to modernise and to explore new forms of production and commercialisation, specifically with regard to the digital economy. It anticipates new markets for the agrifood sector, which it sees as benefitting from improvements and modernisation in Priego's businesses. It is, however, once again on tourism – with the aid of European initiatives and resources – that the greatest hopes are pinned. Attention is drawn to the area's historical and cultural heritage and also to the increased focus on ecological tourism. The values associated with culture, leisure and sport are seen as generating 'positive and inclusive social dynamics'. The development of new technologies and their appropriate use is viewed as fundamental.

When, in May 2023, the conservative Partido Popular was returned to power for a further four years, it was on the basis of what it proudly presented as its list of recent achievements and an ambitious programme for the future. These were characterised by a combination of belief in continuing industrial

---

[229] *EDUSI Priego de Córdoba*, pp. 30–33, 62, 89, 96.

[230] Ibid., p.133.

progress with a concern for quality of life and for the preservation of Priego's cultural heritage. There was emphasis on ecologically sound projects such as the development of the path up the mountain of La Tiñosa and the installation of energy-efficient lighting in Priego, and also on the creation of the sustainable children's traffic park, at a cost of almost a quarter of a million euros, in Calle Joaquín Blume, close to the Ciudad Deportiva Carlos Machado. The council also prided itself on having tackled long-standing thorny issues, notably those of the water company and the restoration of Calle Río, and on the creation of the rich and varied cultural agenda under the umbrella of the Mascarón project.[231]

The council's programme seemed to reflect an understanding of Priego's most pressing needs and a determination to tackle them. Prominent among these demands has been the insistence that Priego should have its own hospital, and it was now promised that within the next four years a new medical centre would eliminate the present dependence on Cabra. This scheme would involve an investment of 10.7 million euros. There were also various proposals for improving the facilities for car parking, including a new car park situated close to the historic centre for visitors to the town. The decision taken at the end of 2022 with regard to the construction of the new stretch of the A333 as it bypasses the narrow and winding gorge at Las Angosturas appears particularly significant. Its route is to be changed in order to permit the thorough investigation and exploitation of the important Roman site which has been discovered at El Cortijo de los Cipreses (see Chapter 1). This seems to be a clear indicator of new priorities and of the belief that fresh discoveries can further enhance Priego's position as potentially one of Andalucía's most important tourist centres.

---

[231] This was the name (meaning literally 'a mask') now given to the prestigious festival of music and dance which had first been introduced in 1948.

Calle Río
This photograph was taken in summer 2023, after the completion of the extensive work carried out on underground drainage and cabling, which had paralysed the area's traffic for over a year. On the left is a statue of Niceto Alcalá-Zamora outside the house where he was born, which now serves as a museum dedicated to his memory. The church in the background is the Iglesia del Carmen. Rebuilt in the late eighteenth century, it marks a period of transition from Baroque to Neoclassical style. *Photograph by Félix Javier Serrano Serrano.*

There remain other areas of which more could, perhaps, be made, including cave systems like the Cueva de los Mármoles, more imaginative exploitation of which could further enrich Priego's varied cultural offering. There are certainly many good reasons why tourism is widely seen to be a vital part of Priego's future. This optimism is given vigorous expression by a representative of Priego's outstanding tourist office:

> I see the future of tourism as offering many opportunities, with a lot of challenges and a great deal of work to be done, but a great

future. I see it as full of hope; it just cannot be otherwise. It has to be carefully planned, with considerable involvement from the people, companies and employees. A great future, but there is a long road ahead of us. And always bearing in mind that the town's tourist activities will allow its citizens to enjoy a better standard of living. I have great expectations.[232]

*

It is axiomatic that any community must to a certain extent be a product of its history. However, in the case of Priego de Córdoba, the truth of this seems to be particularly apparent. The town's pride in its past achievements – reflected in its historical role as a bulwark of Christendom and embodied above all in its wealth of Baroque architecture and in the continuing displays of popular piety which characterise its religious festivals – is central to its present-day existence and its hopes for the future. In some of these respects, Priego has much in common with several other Andalusian towns, but there is much about the character of this community that is distinctive. Its celebrations cannot be compared with those of the great cities for scale and grandeur, but they gain in intimacy and intensity. It is impossible to understand their significance without taking into account the centuries of devotion which lie behind them. Perhaps this also helps to explain the firm belief that Priego's historical background and its cultural and spiritual values will continue to play a fundamental role in the future.

How far Priego's young people really share those traditional values and beliefs is not entirely clear, however, and likewise it seems doubtful whether those who participate in the activities of the *cofradías* do so out of Christian devotion or through respect for the town's cultural heritage. On the other hand, there can be no doubt with regard to the level of awareness which now exists that in order to flourish – or at least hold its own – in the coming

---

[232] José Peláez López, in an interview with the author, September 2022.

decades, Priego must modernise its outlook and explore new opportunities at the same time as preserving pride in its historical achievements.

The observer of Priego's past will be aware, moreover, of a striking anomaly. Between its establishment in the eighth century and its recapture by Christian armies under Alfonso XI in 1341, Priego, or rather madīnat Bāguh, was a Muslim community, which reached the height of its prosperity in the twelfth and early thirteenth centuries. If we are to identify a true golden age in the town's history, it is arguably the latter part of its existence under Islamic rule; and yet, amidst the intense celebration of Priego's Christian heritage, there is scant recognition of these deep Islamic roots. This is hardly surprising in view of the religious and ideological conditions which have prevailed over the past five centuries, but it is an aspect of the town's identity which must not be ignored. The Partido Popular's programme specifically mentioned the acquisition and restoration of the pennant that commemorated the heroism of a member of the Zamorano family (see Chapter 4), and this proudly displayed treasure is dominated by the figure of Santiago (Saint James, often known as 'Matamoros', 'the Moor-Slayer') riding over the broken bodies of Muslim foes. The street layout of the town's historic quarter, the Barrio de la Villa, still reflects that of the old Muslim town, but most of the cultural heritage of those six centuries (and, indeed, that left by the *Morisco* population of the sixteenth century) has been swept away. Important research has been done in recent decades, but it is to be hoped that, in the future, fresh discoveries will fill in some of the gaps in our knowledge of this vitally important aspect of the town's history. Perhaps the new museum, which is eventually to be housed in the restored Montoro-Castilla mill, will make it possible to display more extensive evidence of Priego's illustrious Islamic past alongside the glories of its Christian tradition.

*

Priego continues to hope that its textile and clothing industry will again prosper with the aid of new technology and suitably enterprising investment. What is beyond doubt is that the necessary skills still exist in the community. There are extensive premises in the heart of the old town which once housed a thriving industry and which at present remain unused. There are surely possibilities for development in any of a number of ways, building on this crucial facet of Priego's past. These include clear potential for exploitation as part of the town's tourist offering. At present, in spite of the existence of a small but fascinating museum dedicated to the textile industry, many visitors to Priego remain largely unaware of the town's distinguished industrial past.

*

Today, Priego is best known for its olive oil, and it is on this industry that the town's economic wellbeing largely depends. There is, however, a significant risk in this heavy reliance on the olive monoculture. In the long term, climate change poses a serious threat, but for the immediate future a series of years of increasingly dry weather is already posing serious problems. The water supply is stretched to its limit, an ironic twist, perhaps, for an area which for so long had been known for its rivers and rich agricultural land. In addition, the nature of the agricultural sector, characterised by a predominance of smallholdings owned by individual rural farmers, does not favour the reinvestment of profits, technological innovation or commercialisation. Priego's network of dependent villages has an ageing population (with its consequent social problems) and suffers from a steady haemorrhaging of its younger and more dynamic residents towards the town itself but also further afield. There is a disconcerting sense that many young people are losing belief in their future. The need for education, investment and revitalisation is apparent, and this applies to the villages and rural areas at least as much as to the urban centre. It

POSTSCRIPT: PRIEGO PAST, PRESENT AND FUTURE

is, therefore, encouraging to see Priego's council now expressing its commitment to the development of the villages and recognising the essential role that they have to play in the future. It is vital that this is backed up with increased practical support and real concern for improving the quality of life and the opportunities for employment in these outlying areas.

Priego currently finds itself, as do many other communities in Spain and abroad, at a critical point in its development. It can proudly boast of an illustrious past, which colours its present and will inevitably continue to play an important part in determining its future. However, it now has to face multiple new challenges: economic, social, technological, environmental. It may well be that education (for both the young and adults) – coupled with the encouragement of enterprise and initiative – holds the key.

Select Bibliography

A number of important sources cited in the text are available online.

The complete collection of the periodical Adarve, *covering two periods of its existence (1952–1968 and 1976–2015):*
www.periodicoadarve.com/ficheros/paginas/hemeroteca.htm
More recent numbers are available at:
www.periodicoadarve.com/index.php?page=1

Enrique Alcalá Ortiz has made a wide range of material available on his website http://www.enriquealcalaortiz.com/, including an extensive collection of photographs.

Antiqvitas, *the annual journal published by Priego's Museo Histórico Municipal: www.antiqvitas.es*

Legajos, *the journal published under the auspices of the Municipal Archive of the Ayuntamiento de Priego de Córdoba:*
http://archivopriegodecordoba.com/index.php/revista-legajos

The comprehensive survey EDUSI Priego de Córdoba 2020 containing details of Priego's Urban Development Strategy, published by the Ayuntamiento of Priego de Córdoba under the auspices of the European Fund for Regional Development:
https://www.edusipriegocordoba.org/

*

Of the books and articles listed below, those specific to Priego are in Spanish, but a small number of more general background works in English are also included.

Alcalá Ortiz, Enrique, 1988, 2002, 2008. *Historia de Priego de Andalucía* (3 vols) (Priego de Córdoba: Excmo. Ayuntamiento de Priego de Córdoba).
Alcalá Ortiz, Enrique, 1992. *Cancionero popular de Priego* (vol. 5) (Priego de Córdoba: Excmo. Ayuntamiento de Priego de Córdoba).

Alcalá Ortiz, Enrique, 2004. *Lo que ellos vieron del Priego antiguo* (Priego de Córdoba: Excmo. Ayuntamiento de Priego de Córdoba, Área de Cultura; CajaSur).
Alcalá-Zamora y Ruiz de Tienda, Pedro, 1976. *Apuntes para la historia de Priego*. Prologue by José Valverde Madrid, in *Boletín de la Real Academia de Córdoba de Ciencias, Bellas Letras y Nobles Artes*, 96.
Alférez Molina, Candelaria, 2000. 'Presencia del Tribunal de la Inquisición en la Villa de Priego. Perseguidos y perseguidores', *Legajos*, 4, pp.41–60.
Alférez Molina, Candelaria, 2004. *Priego de Córdoba en la edad moderna: epidemias, hermandades y arte devocional* (Priego de Córdoba: Ayuntamiento de Priego de Córdoba).
Aranda Doncel, Juan, 1984. *Los moriscos en tierra de Córdoba* (Córdoba: Monte de Piedad y Caja de Ahorros de Córdoba).
Arjona Castro, Antonio, 1989. 'La comarca de la Subbética cordobesa durante las invasiones de los almorávides y almohades', *Boletín de la Real Academia de Córdoba*, 117, pp.115–46.
Arjona Castro, Antonio, 1990. 'Arqueología e historia de las torres atalayas de las comarcas de Priego y Alcalá la Real', *Antiqvitas*, 1, pp.32–37.
Barrios Aguilera, Manuel, 2008. *Moriscos de Andalucía* (Granada: CajaGranada – Obra Social).
Cano Montoro, Encarnación, 2012. Published online 2013. *La región de Priego de Córdoba (kūrat Bāguh) en el proceso de formación de al-Andalus (siglos VIII–IX)* (Granada: Editorial de la Universidad de Granada).
Cano Montoro, Encarnación, 2015. *Omeyas, Tribus y Coras. El caso de Bāguh (Priego de Córdoba)* (Jerez de la Frontera: Peripecias Libros, Ediciones Presea S.L.).
Carmona Ávila, Rafael, 1998. 'Priego de Córdoba en la Edad Media: una aproximación histórica y arqueológica', *Antiqvitas*, 9, pp.161–75.
Carmona Ávila, Rafel, 1999. 'La cueva de los Mármoles (Priego de Córdoba): análisis de resultados de una prospección arqueológica superficial', *Antiqvitas*, 10, pp.5–24.
Carmona Ávila, Rafael, 2004. 'El pendón de los Zamorano (Priego de Córdoba): aproximación a una enseña militar bajomedieval de valor excepcional', *Antiqvitas*, 16, pp.131–49.
Carmona Ávila, Rafael, 2005. 'El Palenque (Priego de Córdoba): introducción a su evolución urbana según la aportación de la arqueología y una revisión de las fuentes bibliográficas y documentales', *Antiqvitas*, 17, pp.83–136.
Carmona Ávila, Rafael, 2009. 'La madina andalusí de Bāguh: una aproximación arqueológica', in *XELB: 6° Encontro de Arqueologia del Algarve* (Silves: Camara Municipal de Silves), pp.229–258.
Carmona Ávila, Rafael, 2010. 'Aproximación arqueológica al territorio del

rebelde muladí Ibn Mastana (s. IX d.C.) en la comarca de madīnat Bagūh (Priego de Córdoba)', *Antiqvitas*, 22, pp.141–57.
Carmona Ávila, Rafael, 2012. 'Ascetas, devotos y misticismo islámico: nuevas perspectivas sobre la ocupación de cuevas naturales en madīnat Bagūh (Priego de Córdoba)', *Antiqvitas*, 24, pp.223–64.
Carmona Ávila, 2014. 'La región de Priego de Córdoba (kūrat Bāguh) en el proceso de formación de al-Andalus (siglos VIII–IX): consideraciones en torno a una tesis doctoral', *Antiqvitas*, 26, pp.267–86.
Carmona Ávila, Rafael, 2016. 'La villa romana de Priego de Córdoba', in Rafael Hidalgo Prieto, ed., *Las villas romanas de la Bética, vol.2, catálogo* (Editorial Universidad de Sevilla, 2016), pp.232–41.
Carmona Ávila, Rafael, 2021. 'El castillo de Priego de Córdoba: notas sobre su evolución, descripción y arqueología', *Castillos de España: Monográfico sobre castillos de la provincia de Córdoba*, pp.201–211.
Carmona Ávila, Rafael, and Dolores Luna Osuna, 2007. 'La villa romana de Priego (Córdoba): primeros datos aportados por la Actividad Arqueológica Urgente de C/Carrera de las Monjas, n° 3, de 2007', *Antiqvitas*, 18/19, pp.81–126.
Carmona Ávila, Rafael, and Dolores Luna Osuna, 2010. 'Anotaciones a la villa romana y poblamiento medieval de Priego (Córdoba): resultados del seguimiento realizado al movimiento de tierras previo a la edificación del solar de C/Carrera de las monjas, n° 3', *Antiqvitas*, 22, pp.77–87.
Carmona Ávila, Rafael, Dolores Luna Osuna and Antonio Moreno Rosa, 2002. *Carta Arqueológica Municipal de Priego de Córdoba* (Junta de Andalucía, Consejo de Cultura).
Carr, Matthew, 2017. *Blood and Faith. The Purging of Muslim Spain 1492–1614* (London: Hurst and Company).
Carr, Raymond, 1980. *Modern Spain 1875-1980* (Oxford: Oxford University Press).
Casas Sánchez, José Luis, 2006. *Niceto Alcalá-Zamora y Torres (1877–1949)* (Cabra: Mancomunicad de la Subbética y Diputación de Córdoba).
Caston Boyer, 1985. *La religión en Andalucía (aproximación a la religiosidad popular)* (Sevilla: Editoriales Andaluzas Unidas S.A.).
Cobo Calmaestra, Rafael, 1998, 'Aproximación al problema morisco en Priego de Córdoba (1486–1611)', *Legajos*, 1, pp.7–18.
Cortes Sánchez, Miguel, et al., 2008. 'La investigación sobre El Pirulejo. Una aproximación interdisciplinar', *Antiqvitas*, 20, pp.213–21.
Cuadros Callava, Jesús, 1999. 'Enfrentamiento de la oligarquía prieguense durante la transición a la II República', *Legajos*, 2, pp.37–62.
Cuadros Callava, Jesús, 2019. *La nada y el silencio. Represalias políticas y sociales en Priego de Córdoba, 1936–39* (Sevilla: Aconcagua Libros).

Del Caño Pozo, José Francisco, 2018. *La destrucción de la obra educativa de la República en Priego de Córdoba (1936–39)* (Sevilla: Aconcagua Libros).
Drayson, Elizabeth, 2017. *The Moor's Last Stand. How Seven Centuries of Muslim Rule in Spain Came to an End* (Northampton, Massachusetts: Interlink Books).
Durán Alcalá, Francisco, and Carmen Ruiz Barrientos, 2010. *Casa-museo de don Niceto Alcalá-Zamora y Torres de Priego de Córdoba*, 2nd edition (Córdoba: Diputación de Córdoba; Patronato Municipal Niceto Alcalá-Zamora y Torres; Cajasur).
Forcada Serrano, Miguel, 1992. *Toros en Priego (en el centenario de la construcción de la plaza)* (Córdoba: Caja Provincial de Ahorros de Córdoba).
Forcada Serrano, Miguel, 2000. *Historia de la Hermandad de la Santa Vera Cruz y Nuestro Padre Jesús en la Columna* (Córdoba: Monte de Piedad y Caja de Ahorros de Córdoba).
Forcada Serrano, Miguel, 2013. 'El patrimonio perdido de Priego y las cofradías', *La crónica de Córdoba y sus pueblos*, IX (Diputación de Córdoba, Departamento de Ediciones y Publicaciones), pp.113–24.
Forcada Serrano, Miguel, 2016. *La industria textil del algodón en Priego de Córdoba. El sueño imposible de una ciudad industrial en el corazón de Andalucía* (Priego de Córdoba: edición del autor).
Forcada Serrano, Miguel, 2018. *Zamoranos. Historia y vida* (Priego de Córdoba: edición del autor).
Forcada Serrano, Miguel, et al., 2000. *A. Lozano Sidro. Vida, obra y catálogo general* (Ayuntamiento de Priego de Córdoba; Obra Social y Cultural de CajaSur).
Gómez Ropero, Manuel, et al., 2003. *Geografía, Naturaleza, Historia, Arte, Etnografía. Priego de Córdoba: guía multidisciplinar de la ciudad y su territorio*, 3rd ed. (Priego de Córdoba: Ayuntamiento de Priego de Córdoba, Diputación de Córdoba).
González Zymla, Herbert, Adolfo Lozano Sidro, in Real Academia de la Historia, *Diccionario Biográfico electrónico* (http://dbe.rah.es/).
Gutiérrez López, José A., ed., 2014. *Priego de Córdoba, sus hermandades y cofradías* (Priego de Córdoba: Agrupación de Hermandades y Cofradías de Semana Santa).
Lara Martín-Portugués, 1989. 'Del Jaén de 1823. El primer sueño liberal'. *Boletín del Instituto de Estudios Giennenses* (Jaén: Diputación Provincial de Jaén), pp.9–28.
Leiva Briones, Fernando, 2014. *Fuente-Tójar (Córdoba): aproximación a su arqueología e historia antigua* (Fuente-Tójar, Córdoba: Ayuntamiento de Fuente-Tójar).
Leiva Briones, Fernando, 2019. *La Guerra Civil (1936–1939) en el municipio*

cordobés de Fuente-Tójar según los testimonios orales, escritos y materiales (Córdoba: Diputación de Córdoba).

López de Varga Machuca, Tomás, 2008. *Diccionario geográfico de Andalucía* Ed. Cristina Seguía Graíño (Córdoba: Diputación Provincial de Códoba).

López Calvo, Manuel, 1988. *Priego, caciquismo y resignación popular (1868–1923). Aproximación a la historia de un pueblo andaluz durante la Restauración* (Córdoba: Centro Asociado de Córdoba – UNED).

Madoz, Pascual, 1845–1850. *Diccionario geográfico-estadístico-histórico de España y sus posesiones de ultramar* (vol. XIII) (Madrid: Est. Literario-Tipográfico de P. Madoz y L. Sagasti, 1846).

Martínez Enamorado, Virgilio, 1998. 'Sobre Madinat Baguh: aspectos historiográficos de una ciudad andalusí y su alfoz', *Antiquitas*, 9, pp.129–50.

Martínez Sevilla, Francisco, 2010. 'Un taller neolítico de brazaletes de piedra en la cueva de los Mármoles', *Antiquitas*, 22, pp.35–55.

Matilla Rivadeneyra, Antonio, 2022. *La industria textil en Priego de Córdoba* (Priego de Córdoba: Asociación de Amigos de Priego de Córdoba).

Mendoza Carreño, Manuel, 1984. *José Luis Gamiz Valverde: Priego, historia de una época* (Córdoba: Ediciones El Almendro).

Moreno Rosa, Antonio, 1992. 'Pinturas rupestres paleolíticas en la Cueva de Cholones (Subbéticas Cordobesas)', *Antiquitas*, 3, pp.8–22.

Morgado Rodríguez, Antonio, Rafael Mª Martínez Sánchez and Rafael Carmona Ávila, 2015. 'Puntualizaciones sobre el tránsito V-IV milenio cal.AC en la Alta Andalucía. El primer asentamiento en el casco urbano de Priego de Córdoba', *Antiquitas*, 27, pp.31–48.

Muñiz Jaén, Ignacio, 2009. *Apuntes para una historia silenciada. Luchas campesinas en Andalucía: Almedinilla durante la Guerra Civil. Oikos, n° 1.* (Almedinilla: Ayuntamiento de Almedinilla; Ecomuseo del Río Caicena; Junta de Andalucía).

Osuna Luque, R, 2003. *Instituto Fernando III El Santo, 50 aniversario, 1953–2003* (Publicación del propio Instituto).

Peláez del Rosal, Manuel, 1990. *La Inmaculada Concepción. Patrona de Priego* (Priego de Córdoba: Excmo. Ayuntamiento de Priego de Córdoba).

Peláez del Rosal, Manuel, 2000. 'Una fundación docente de San Juan de Ávila y de la Condesa de Feria: el colegio de San Nicasio de Priego', *Fuente del Rey*, 197, pp.5–9.

Peláez del Rosal, Manuel, 2005. *La Calle del Río de Priego de Córdoba* (Priego de Córdoba: Revista Fuente del Rey).

Peláez del Rosal, Manuel, 2006. 'El convento de Clarisas de la villa de Priego (1617-1872): aspectos económicos, jurídicos, demográficos, artísticos y culturales', in *El Franciscanismo en Andalucía: Clarisas, Concepcionistas y Terciarias Regulares, Conferencias del X Curso de Verano*,

Priego de Córdoba, 26 a 30 de julio de 2004 (Córdoba, 2006), pp.617–722.

Peláez del Rosal, Manuel, 2014. *El antiguo convento de San Francisco de Priego de Córdoba (Hotel-Hospedería San Francisco)* (Priego de Córdoba: Asociación de Amigos de Priego de Córdoba).

Peláez del Rosal, Manuel, articles on Juan de Dios Santaella and Pedro Alcalá-Zamora Ruiz de la Tienda, in Real Academia de la Historia, *Diccionario Biográfico electrónico* (http://dbe.rah.es/).

Peláez del Rosal, Manuel, and María Concepción Quintanilla Raso, 1977. *Priego de Córdoba en la Edad Media* (Salamanca).

Peláez del Rosal, Manuel, and Jesús Rivas Carmona, 1980. *Priego de Córdoba: guía histórica y artística de la ciudad* (Salamanca: Excmo. Ayuntamiento de Priego de Córdoba).

Phillips, William D., and Carla Rahn Phillips, 2010. *A Concise History of Spain* (Cambridge: Cambridge University Press).

Raya Raya, Mª de Los Ángeles, articles on Francisco Hurtado Izquierdo, Jerónimo Sánchez de Rueda, Francisco Javier Pedrajas and Remigio del Mármol, in Real Academia de la Historia, *Diccionario Biográfico electrónico* (http://dbe.rah.es/).

Ross, Christopher J., 2009. *Spain since 1812. Modern History for Modern Languages* (Abingdon: Routledge).

Quesada Marco, Sebastián, 2007. *Historia social y económica de Andalucía* (Úbeda, Jaén: El Olivo).

Rubio Valverde, Manuel, 2020. 'El territorio de Zagrilla en la Prehistoria. El poblamiento primitivo', in Manuel Peláez del Rosal, ed., *Pinceladas sobre Zagrilla* (Priego de Córdoba: Asociación de Amigos de Priego de Córdoba), pp.43–50.

Ruiz-Burruecos Sánchez, Maximiliano, 2000. 'La instrucción primaria en Priego durante el siglo XIX y el primer tercio del XX', *Legajos*, 3, pp.69–92.

Ruiz Mata, José, 2022. *Breve Historia de Andalucía. Tomo 1: de la Prehistoria a los visigodos* (Jerez de la Frontera: Tierra de Nadie Editores).

Sánchez López et al., 1988. *La confección al sur de Córdoba* (Córdoba: Servicio de Publicaciones de la Universidad de Córdoba. Excmo. Ayuntamiento de Priego de Córdoba).

Such, Peter, 2020. *Chronicle of King Pedro by Pero López de Ayala* (Liverpool: Liverpool University Press).

Thomas, Hugh, 2003. *The Spanish Civil War*, 4th ed. (London: Penguin Books).

Tremlett, Giles, 2022. *España. A Brief History of Spain* (London and New York: Bloomsbury).

Valverde Castilla, José Tomás, *Memorias de un alcalde*. Prólogo de José María Pemán, 1961 (Madrid: Editorial Escelicer).

Vera Aranda, Ángel Luis, 1993. 'Aproximación a la evolución urbana de Priego de Córdoba', *Revista de Estudios Andaluces*, 19, pp.129–74.

Vera Rodríguez, Juan Carlos et al., 1999. 'La cueva de Los Mármoles (Priego de Córdoba): análisis de resultados de una prospección arqueológica superficial', *Antiquitas*, 10, pp.5–24.

Index to Names of People and Places

Abbāsids: 19, 25
'Abd Alāh al-Bayyāsī: 33
'Abd al-Malik al-Muẓaffar: 26
'Abd al-Raḥmān I: 19
'Abd al-Raḥmān III: 23, 25
Adarve: 31, 110, 112, 144
Adelaida Arjona Castro: 147
Adolfo Lozano Sidro: 114, 116, 117, 170, 171, 177
Aguilar (family, lordship): 40, 44, 45, 49, 50
Aguilar de la Frontera: 40
Aḥmad ibn Qāsim al-Kalbī: 25
Alarcos: 32
Albayate (Sierra): 1, 30
Alcalá de Benzaide (Alcalá La Real): 35, 36, 39
Alcalá la Real: 3, 20, 22, 24, 35, 42, 47, 61, 65, 91, 96, 113, 169
Alcalá-Zamora (family): 97, 108, 122, 170
Alcaudete: 12, 33, 35, 37, 40, 41, 95
alcazaba: 28, 29, 46
Alejandro Farnesio (Cardinal): 61
Alfonso VIII: 32, 33
Alfonso X: 36
Alfonso XI: 37, 38, 39, 40, 44, 45, 46, 56, 66, 106, 121, 125, 185
Alfonso XII: 106
Alfonso XIII: 121, 125
Alfonso de Aguilar (Don): 43, 45, 62
Alfonso Fernández de Córdoba (Don): 41, 42

al-Ḥakam II: 25
Alhóndiga (La) (see also El Pósito): 54
Alhucemas: 24
'Āliya: 24
al-Manṣūr: 25
Almedinilla: 11, 13, 15, 30, 45, 80, 100, 104, 136, 192
Almendros (Los): 15, 166, 174
Almogáveres (Los): 0
Almohads: 27, 29, 30, 31, 32, 34, 35
Almoravids: 27
Almudena Grandes: – 138
al-Muqaddasī: 23
al-Mu'tamid ibn 'Abbād: 26
Alonso de Mena: 74
Alonso González Bailén: 56
Alpujarra (mountains): 44
al-Qasar (alcazaba): 28, 29, 46
al-'Uḏhrī: 22
Álvaro de Luna: 42
Angosturas (Las): 1, 2, 5, 10, 13, 14, 30, 110, 111, 142, 166, 182
Antonio Povedano: 171
Antonio Zarco: 171
Archduke Charles (pretender to the Spanish throne): 78
Arabs: 20, 21
Arenas: 36
Arrimadizo (El): 17, 20
Astigis (Écija): 12
Atarazana (district of Priego): 178
Avenida de España (Priego) 147, 164

195

INDEX TO NAMES OF PEOPLE AND PLACES

Azores: 14

Baena: 20
Baetica: 1, 12, 13
Baeza: 33, 34
Bailén: 56, 95
Banū Mastana: 24, 27
Barcas: 41, 43
Barcelona: 110, 119, 131, 142, 156
Barrio de la Morería: 29
Barrio de la Villa: 7, 22, 28, 29, 31, 60, 83, 166
Bastetani: 9
Berbers: 20, 21, 26, 27
Berenguer (General Dámaso) 125
Boabdil: 43, 48

Cabezuelas (del Tarajal)(Las): 8, 9
Cabra: 17, 20, 22, 112, 145, 169, 182, 190
Cádiz: 78, 81, 95, 96
Calle Carrera de las Monjas: (Priego) 15, 16, 54, 59, 103, 106, 116, 134, 143, 157
Calle Carrera del Águila (Priego): 136
Calle Cava (Priego): 7, 67, 123, 142
Calle de La Libertad: 103, 158
Calle del 18 de Julio: 158
Calle Héroes de Toledo: 157
Calle Joaquín Blume (Priego): 182
Calle José Antonio 143, 157
Calle Málaga (Priego): 54
Calle Molinos (Priego): 110
Calle Prim: 106
Calle Ramón y Cajal (Priego): 16, 122, 142, 163
Calle Ribera (Priego): 54, 88, 158, 166
Calle Río (Priego): 8, 54,56, 82, 112, 115, 122, 127, 130, 134-135, 146-147, 157, 170, 176, 182-183
Calle San Luis (Priego) 128
Calle San Marcos (Priego): 142

Calle Tercia (Priego): 7
Calle Trasmonjas (Priego): 7
Calvario (height of): 54, 59, 75, 86, 90, 166, 177
Calvario (La Virgen del) (ermita): 59, 75, 86, 90, 166, 177
campiña cordobesa: 107, 118
Campo Nubes: 123
Cañoscorrientes: 14
Cañuelo (El): 9, 14, 100, 110, 119, 161
Caracuel (General Manuel López) 04, 105, 106
Carcabuey: 5, 13, 16, 47, 103
Carlos I: 52, 63
Carlos II: 67, 77
Carlos III: 77
Carlos IV: 94
Carlos Machado: 178, 182
Carlos María Isidro: 100
Carlos Valverde López: 108, 113, 114, 117, 118, 119, 178
Carnicerías Reales: 55, 56, 57, 90, 171, 176
Carrasca (La): 134, 135
Castil de Campos: 30, 80, 100, 104, 110, 119, 132, 168, 180
Castilla family: 144
Castillejos: 10, 12
Castillo de Locubín: 37
Castro del Río: 118
Catalina Fernández de Córdoba (Doña): 51
Cataluña: 67,118, 140, 144, , 154, 159
Catholic Monarchs: 43, 44, 48, 50
'Cencerro': 138
Cerro de la Cruz: 11, 12
Cerro de las Cabezas: 11, 14, 136
Cerro de las Pollicas: 9
Cerro de las Viñas: 1
Cerro del Cercado: 4
Cerro del Torreón: 6
Cerro Lucerico: 12
Cerro Severo: 8, 10

196

INDEX TO NAMES OF PEOPLE AND PLACES

Charles V (Holy Roman Emperor;
  see also Carlos I): 52
Cholones (Cueva de): 2, 5, 36, 192
Cholones (Loma de):2
Ciudad Deportiva Carlos Machado:
  165, 178, 182
Collejares (Los): 41
Compás (El): 58
Cordillera Subbética: 1
Córdoba (city): 12, 19, 23-26, 29, 33,
  34, 43, 64, 93, 95, 100, 103, 106, 126,
  136, 141, 144
Cortijo de los Cipreses: 13, 182
Cuarenta (Cueva de los): 5
Cubé (La): 18, 30, 37

Despeñaperros (pass): 32, 33
Diego Fernández: 44

Egabrum (Cabra): 17, 22
Elvira (Kūra Ilbīra): .25, 27
Emilio Fernández: 135
Encarnación (La) (arch of): 46, 82
Enrique II: 40
Enrique IV: 43
Enrique Cabello Povedano: 134
Esparragal (El): 6, 100, 119, 180
Espartero (General Baldomero): 103
Espejo: 118

Felipe (Philippe) V: 77, 78
Felipe González: 157
Felipe III: 65, 66
Felipe IV: 66, 67
Fernán Delgadillo: 39, 40
Fernandez de Córdoba (family): 40
Fernando Berdugo: 98
Fernando III: 27, 33, 34, 39, 40, 47,
  139, 147
Fernando VII: 94, 95, 96, 100
Fernando of Aragón (husband of
  Isabel I; see also Catholic
  Monarchs): 43, 48, 49,50

Francisco Adame: 132
Francisco del Castillo: 56, 57
Francisco Hurtado Izquierdo: 85, 86,
  193
Francisco Javier Pedrajas: 86, 87, 89,
  193
Francisco Ruiz Santaella: 114, 115
Franco (General Francisco): 131, 135,
  136, 144, 150, 157, 167, 170, 172
Fray Luis de Granada: 59
Fuente Barea: 14
Fuente de la Salud (El Cañuelo): 14
Fuente de la Salud (Priego): 56, 110,
  123
Fuente del Triunfo: 104
Fuente del Rey: 16, 28, 46, 55, 56, 78,
  88, 89, 90, 91, 96, 104, 177
Fuente-Tójar: 10, 11, 80, 100, 104, 119,
  120, 136, 138

Gómez Damas (General Miguel): 103
Gonzalo Fernández de Córdoba: 40,
  41, 45, 46
Gonzalo Ruiz de Figueroa: 50
Granada: 26, 27, 34, 36, 37-38, 41-44,
  46, 48-49, 50, 52-53, 60, 63, 85, 93,
  99, 104, 113, 141
Gregorio Alcalá-Zamora y Caracuel:
  105, 106
Guadalquivir (river): 1, 8, 107, 141

Higueras (Las): 128
Hishām II: 25
Hispania Ulterior: 12
Historians: Rafael Carmona Ávila,
  Miguel Forcada Serrano, Manuel
  Peláez del Rosal, Enrique Alcalá
  Ortiz: 172
Horconera (Sierra): 1, 3, 5, 24, 30
Hotel-Museo Patria Chica: 177
Huerta Anguita: 7, 30
Huerta de las Infantas (see also
  Recreo de Castilla): 144, 177

INDEX TO NAMES OF PEOPLE AND PLACES

Huerta de las Palomas: 163
Huerta Palacio: 55, 155

Ibn Abī 'Āmir (al-Manṣūr): 25
Ibn al-Jaṭīb: 21
Ibn 'Ammār: 26
Ibn Hayyān: 24
Iliturgicola: 11, 12
Indalecio Prieto: 126
Ipolcobulcoba: 12, 16, 17
Isabel I (see also Catholic Monarchs): 43, 48, 49
Isabel II: 100, 101, 104, 105, 116
Isabel de Trujillo: 64

Jaén: 1, 32, 33, 35, 41, 53, 57, 98, 108, 138
Jardín del Moro: 30
Jerónimo Molina Sánchez: 110
Jerónimo Sánchez de Rueda: 85, 86
Jesús Cuadros: 172
José Álvarez Cubero: 89
José Calvo Sotelo: 131
José Carrillo Montoro: 141
José Fernando Berdugo: 98
José Linares Montero: 150
José Luis Gamiz: 143, 146
José Luis Machado: 178
José Ramón Matilla: 110
José Tomás (síndico): 97
José Tomás Valverde: 120, 121, 123, 126, 132
Juan II: 42
Juan Álvarez de Mendizábal: 101
Juan Calvo Moreno: 106
Juan de Austria (Don): 63
Juan de Dios Santaella: 84, 85, 86
Juan de Herrera: 68
Juan Manuel Sánchez y Gutiérrez de Castro: 108
Juan Martín de Zamorano: 49, 50
Juan Nepomuceno Prats (Field Marshal): 99

Juana Enríquez de Ribera (Doña): 68

La Asunción (Nuestra Señora de) (church of): 18, 29, 58, 82, 85, 86, 87, 88, 90, 164, 177
La Aurora (Nuestra Señora de) (church of): 18, 29, 47, 55, 59, 60, 62, 84, 85, 86, 90, 177
Lagunillas (Las): 5, 30, 45, 123, 175, 180
La Moraleda (district of Priego): 146
la Morería: 29, 63, 65
Las Mercedes (church of): 59, 86, 90
La Tiñosa (mountain): 1, 31, 175, 182
La Trinidad (church of): 128
La Vega (industrial area): 160, 166
Lagunillas (Las): 5, 30, 45, 123, 175, 180
Linares Montero (José, Francisco, Antonio): 142
Llano de la Iglesia: 55, 90, 96
Llanos (Los): 9, 12, 13
Loja: 27, 34, 43
Louis XIV (king of France): 77
Lucena: 20, 85, 169, 176
Luis Alcalá-Zamora: 104
Luis García Ochoa: 171
Lukk (Luque): 24

madīnat al-Zahrā: 25
madīnat Bāguh: 16, 18, 19, 21, 22, 23, 24, 25, 26, 27, 30, 31, 32, 33, 34, 37, 38, 147, 185
madīnat Gharnāṭah (Medina Garnata): 26
Majalcorón: 45
Málaga: 23, 54, 65, 67, 93, 104, 120
Mallorca: 154
Marcos Sánchez de Rueda: 85
María Cristina (de Borbón, mother of Isabel II): 100
María de la Purificación Castillo Bidaburu: 129

INDEX TO NAMES OF PEOPLE AND PLACES

Mariana of Austria: 67
Mármoles (Cueva de los): 2, 4, 5, 7, 30, 183
Marquis of Priego: 50, 57, 80, 96
Martos: 34, 37
Medina Sidonia: 21
Medinaceli (duke, Duchy of): 50, 80, 96, 97, 103, 118
Mérida: 15, 141
Montefrío: 43, 45, 62
Montilla: 44, 50, 118
Montoro-Castilla (family): 176
Moriscos: 46, 49, 52, 54, 62, 63, 64, 65, 66, 81
Muḥammad I: 21, 36, 37
Muḥammad II: 36
Muḥammad VIII: 41
Murcielaguina (Cueva de la): 2, 5, 7, 10, 14

Navas de Tolosa (Las): 32
Nicasio (San) (Saint Nicaise) (patron saint of Priego): 42,78
nicetistas: 122 127, 132
Niceto Alcalá-Zamora: 108, 112, 113, 114, 122, 125-130, 134, 139, 140, 144, 165, 170, 183
Nuestra Señora de las Angustias (church of): 90, 97, 105
Nuestra Señora del Carmen (church of): 86, 90. 108, 143, 152
Nuestra Señora del Carmen: 86, 90, 143

Pablo Gámiz Luque: 151
Palenque (El): 7, 15, 18, 30, 55, 90, 113, 127, 135, 147, 165, 167
Paseíllo (El): 148
Paseo de Colombia: 112, 123
Pedro (Prince, brother of Sancho IV): 37
Pedro Alcalá-Zamora: 58, 88, 92, 93, 95, 99, 101

Pedro Ansúrez: 26
Pedro Fernández de Córdoba (died in 1455): 42, 43
Pedro Fernández de Córdoba (1470-1517): 44, 49, 50, 57
Pedro Morales Serrano: 140
Pedro Ruiz de Córdoba: 37
Pedro Sobrados: 173
Pedro (King) ('the Cruel'): 40
Peñas Doblas: 30
Phoenicians: 8, 13
Pirulejo (El): 3, 7
Plaza de Andalucía (Priego): 88, 158, 166
Plaza de la Constitución (Priego): 148
Plaza de los Escribanos (also Plaza del Llano): 55, 82, 90, 164
Poleo (El): 128, 134
Pósito (El): 54, 55, 56, 90, 113, 127, 128, 135
Primo de Rivera (Captain General Miguel): 121, 123, 125, 134
Puerta del Agua: 68, 88
Puerta del Sol: 18, 29, 46, 90

Qal'at Astalīr (also Alcalá la Real):20, 22, 24, 35, 36
Queipo de Llano (General Gonzalo): 132, 158

Rábita (La): 45
Rafael de las Morenas (Lieutenant Colonel): 136
Rafael del Riego (General): 97-98
Rafael Molina Sánchez: 110
Rayya: 23
Recreo de Castilla (see also Huerta de las Infantas): 144, 177
Reina: 21
Remigio del Mármol: 86, 88, 91, 96
Ribarăs: 24
Roldán Écija (Lieutenant): 132
Ruedo (El) (Almedinilla): 13,15

199

Ruedo (El) (area around Priego): 45

Sa'īd ibn Walid ibn Mastana: 24
Saint Francis of Assisi: 57
Salado (river): 1, 2, 3, 18, 24, 30, 38, 41, 110
San Antonio (convent, church of) (see also Santa Clara): 59, 68, 90, 105
San Antonio Abad (ermita): 59
San Bernardo (arch): 46
San Esteban (convent of) (see also San Francisco): 51, 57, 70, 90, 96
San Francisco (convent): 95, 96, 97, 98, 102, 103, 147, 177
San Francisco (church): ... 58, 62, 72, 75, 79, 85, 86, 90, 147
San Ildefonso: 42
San Juan de Ávila: 59
San Juan de Dios (hospital of): 69, 78, 86
San Luis (chapel): 62, 68,
San Luis (factory): 111, 119
San Luis (cemetery): 112
San Marcos (church of): 90
San Nicasio (*ermita*, chapel of): 47, 55, 60, 62, 85
San Onofre (hospice of) (see also San Juan de Dios): 68, 90
San Pedro (*ermita*, church, convent of): 18, 29, 47, 68, 70, 85, 86, 90, 102, 105, 112, 127, 166, 168
Sancho IV: 36, 37, 38
Sanjurjo (General José): 126
Santa Ana (gate, arch): 18, 29, 46, 82, 90, 164
Santa Clara (convent of): 68, 69, 86, 90
Santiago (Saint James, patron saint of Spain): 49, 185
Santiago (church of): 18, 29, 47, 58, 62, 164

Santo Cristo del Humilladero (*ermita*): 59
Sevilla: 4, 26, 29, 33, 81, 93, 126, 131, 132, 141
Sierra de los Judíos: 2, 5
Sierra Gallinera: 5
Sierra Leones: 14, 24
Sierra Morena: 32
Sileras: 24, 45, 100
Sosontigi: 12

Tajo (El): 22, 28, 31, 90
Tarajal (El): 8, 9
Tāriq ibn Ziyād: 9
Tartessos: 8, 9, 10
Teatro Victoria: 166
Teodosio Sánchez de Rueda: 85
Tiñosa (castle): 1, 31, 35, 36, 175, 182
Tomás Jerónimo Pedrajas: 85
Tomás López: 93
Tomás Villén Roldán ('Cencerro'): 138
Torre Alta: 8, 9, 12, 14, 24
Trent: 52, 60, 69
Turdetani: 9

'Umar ibn Ḥafṣūn: 23, 24
Umayyads: 19, 24

Valverde (family): 108, 122, 177
valverdistas: 122, 126-127
Venancio Blanco: 171
Vichira (Llano de): 3
Virgen de la Cabeza: 86, 146

Zagra: 39
Zagrilla (river): 24, 41
Zagrilla (village): 2, 30, 36, 100 121, 169, 180
Zamora: 39

www.ingramcontent.com/pod-product-compliance
Lightning Source LLC
Chambersburg PA
CBHW050551160426
43199CB00015B/2617